A488

INDIAN VEGETARIAN COOKBOOK

INDIAN VEGETARIAN COOKBOOK

Tarla Dalal

HAMLYN

LONDON · NEW YORK · SYDNEY · TORONTO

Back cover shows Vegetable Ring (page 31),
Bean Hotpot (page 55) and Green Peas
Renedy (page 102)

Cover and inside photography by Bob Komar
Illustrations by Sue Lines

Published by Hamlyn Publishing
a division of The Hamlyn Publishing Group Limited
Bridge House, London Road, Twickenham, Middlesex, England
© Copyright The Hamlyn Publishing Group Limited 1983

Third impression 1985
ISBN 0 600 32243 2

Set in Monophoto Apollo by
Servis Filmsetting Limited, Manchester, England
Printed in Italy

Contents

Useful Facts and Figures

Notes on metrication

In this book quantities are given in metric and Imperial measures. Exact conversion from Imperial to metric measures does not usually give very convenient working quantities and so the metric measures have been rounded off into units of 25 grams. The table below shows the recommended equivalents.

Ounces	Approx g to nearest whole figure	Recommended conversion to nearest unit of 25	Ounces	Approx g to nearest whole figure	Recommended conversion to nearest unit of 25
1	28	25	11	312	300
2	57	50	12	340	350
3	85	75	13	368	375
4	113	100	14	396	400
5	142	150	15	425	425
6	170	175	16 (1 lb)	454	450
7	198	200	17	482	475
8	227	225	18	510	500
9	255	250	19	539	550
10	283	275	20 ($1\frac{1}{4}$ lb)	567	575

Note: When converting quantities over 20 oz first add the appropriate figures in the centre column, then adjust to the nearest unit of 25. As a general guide, 1 kg (1000 g) equals 2.2 lb or about 2 lb 3 oz. This method of conversion gives good results in nearly all cases, although in certain pastry and cake recipes a more accurate conversion is necessary to produce a balanced recipe.

Liquid measures The millilitre has been used in this book and the following table gives a few examples.

Imperial	Approx ml to nearest whole figure	Recom- mended ml	Imperial	Approx ml to nearest whole figure	Recom- mended ml
$\frac{1}{4}$ pint	142	150 ml	1 pint	567	600 ml
$\frac{1}{2}$ pint	283	300 ml	$1\frac{1}{2}$ pints	851	900 ml
$\frac{3}{4}$ pint	425	450 ml	$1\frac{3}{4}$ pints	992	1000 ml (1 litre)

Spoon measures All spoon measures given in this book are level unless otherwise stated.

Can sizes At present, cans are marked with the exact (usually to the nearest whole number) metric equivalent of the Imperial weight of the contents, so we have followed this practice when giving can sizes.

Oven temperatures

The table below gives recommended equivalents.

	°C	°F	Gas Mark
Very cool	110	225	$\frac{1}{4}$
	120	250	$\frac{1}{2}$
Cool	140	275	1
	150	300	2
Moderate	160	325	3
	180	350	4
Moderately hot	190	375	5
	200	400	6
Hot	220	425	7
	230	450	8
Very hot	240	475	9

Notes for American and Australian users

In America the 8-oz measuring cup is used. In Australia metric measures are now used in conjunction with the standard 250-ml measuring cup. The Imperial pint, used in Britain and Australia, is 20 fl oz, while the American pint is 16 fl oz. It is important to remember that the Australian tablespoon differs from both the British and American tablespoons; the table below gives a comparison. The British standard tablespoon, which has been used throughout this book, holds 17.7 ml, the American 14.2 ml, and the Australian 20 ml. A teaspoon holds approximately 5 ml in all three countries.

British	American	Australian
1 teaspoon	1 teaspoon	1 teaspoon
1 tablespoon	1 tablespoon	1 tablespoon
2 tablespoons	3 tablespoons	2 tablespoons
$3\frac{1}{2}$ tablespoons	4 tablespoons	3 tablespoons
4 tablespoons	5 tablespoons	$3\frac{1}{2}$ tablespoons

An Imperial/American guide to solid and liquid measures

Imperial	American	Imperial	American
Solid measures		**Liquid measures**	
1 lb butter or		$\frac{1}{4}$ pint liquid	$\frac{2}{3}$ cup liquid
margarine	2 cups	$\frac{1}{2}$ pint	$1\frac{1}{4}$ cups
1 lb flour	4 cups	$\frac{3}{4}$ pint	2 cups
1 lb granulated		1 pint	$2\frac{1}{2}$ cups
or caster sugar	2 cups	$1\frac{1}{2}$ pints	$3\frac{3}{4}$ cups
1 lb icing sugar	3 cups	2 pints	5 cups ($2\frac{1}{2}$
8 oz rice	1 cup		pints)

Note: When making any of the recipes in this book, only follow one set of measures as they are not interchangeable.

Introduction

In India cooking is an art and a tradition handed down from generation to generation, from mother to daughter. Until the advent of cookbooks, all cookery instruction was oral and practical and, whereas certain items like dals, flour and rice were measured, important flavouring ingredients (like spices and masalas) were added according to individual judgement. In fact, until quite recently it was not uncommon for locally published cookbooks to mention ingredients like ginger, chillies and spices without giving any exact quantities. As a result, dishes made from the same list of ingredients showed marked variations in taste from family to family and region to region. Slight variations do not always make the dishes less tasty and hopefully you will feel encouraged to experiment with the recipes in this book.

The parts of India which have a strongly vegetarian population naturally offer a wide selection of vegetarian fare, but in Bengal and coastal areas where fish is plentiful, vegetable dishes tend to be supplementary to the main diet and there are few specialities. However, the popular cuisine of the Punjabis, a vigorous and zestful people, includes both vegetarian and non-vegetarian specialities. With greater mobility people now have an increased awareness and appreciation of foods and dishes from other parts of the country. It is no surprise, therefore, that traditional family cooking is gradually being influenced and altered. The British introduced vegetable cutlets many years ago when they entertained their strictly vegetarian Indian guests and today, ingredients like bread, butter, cheese and Western seasonings such as tomato ketchup are increasingly being used in Indian cooking – even methods like baking are becoming popular. Many of the recipes also reflect these new trends which are developing in Indian cooking.

Despite changes of this sort, it is perhaps the special ingredients that make Indian cooking stand out from the cuisine of other countries. Ghee, for example, is a form of clarified butter which is widely used. However, because of its high cost, ghee made from butter is gradually being replaced by hydrogenated vegetable oils which are known as 'vegetable ghee'. Groundnut and other oils are also used for cooking in many parts of India. Dahi is another common ingredient and in its place, natural yogurt has been specified in the recipes. Other distinctive ingredients made from milk are paneer and khoya. Although the use of spices is common throughout the Orient and coconut is used in coastal areas and islands like Ceylon, the manner in which they are used in India is quite distinct. The numerous combinations of spices and masalas are important for the flavour of the finished dish and the fresher the masalas the better the results. A wide variety of lentils and dals are also used – moong, toovar, urad, gram and masoor dal are just a few of the more common types.

In India, a great deal of importance is attached to food and eating, and in the past the preparation of meals has tended to be a leisurely and long drawn out affair. However, times and tastes are changing. Amongst other things time-saving methods and short cuts are now important to the Indian housewife. Bearing this in mind, all the recipes in this book are extremely easy to follow and although the ingredients list may seem a little formidable at first you will find that the following basic items will cover the spice combinations for most of the recipes – garlic, coriander seeds, cumin seeds, red chillies and chilli powder, cinnamon, cloves, black pepper, cardamom and ginger. I am sure you will find the scope for experimenting with different ingredients and spice combinations an exciting prospect and worthwhile experience. I wish you good eating and many moments of happiness.

Kitchen Equipment

In keeping with the changing times, many urban Indian kitchens now have modern conveniences like refrigerators, pressure cookers, liquidisers, grinders and gas ovens. In addition, traditional equipment and utensils are invariably present. Some of the traditional equipment required for the recipes is described below along with suggested modern alternatives.

For grinding purposes, the pestle and mortar are used for small quantities and a rough-surfaced, black stone grinding slab with a stone roller is used for larger quantities and pastes. Whereas hand grinding gives better results, the electric grinder or liquidiser saves time and hard work. In either case, masalas ground just before they are to be used bring out the best flavour in any dish.

Chapatis and parathas are traditionally rolled out on a circular wooden rolling board (known as a 'patla') using a rolling pin ('velan') which is thicker in the centre than it is at the ends. The rolled-out breads are cooked on a slightly curved iron plat – a 'tava'. They are turned during cooking with the help of a long pair of metal tongs, with flat ends which give a good grip, and these are known as 'chipya'. Instead of these items, a rolling pin can be used and the breads can be cooked in a heavy-based frying pan or griddle with the help of a spatula.

Deep frying is done in a 'kadhai' which is a wide-mouthed metal vessel similar to a chinese wok. The deep-fried food is removed from the ghee or oil with the help of a slightly curved perforated ladle with a long handle – a 'jhara'. The jhara doubles up as a sieve for dropping batter into the fat for making bundis (page 116). A pan designed for deep frying can be used instead of the kadhai and a slotted spoon can be used to replace the jhara.

Traditions and Menus

Most Indians serve their meals on flat circular plates with shallow rims. These are known as 'thalis' and are made either of brass (tinned inside) or stainless steel or, for the well-to-do, of silver. The liquid foods such as dals or curries are poured into cylindrical bowls known as 'katoris' and these are arranged either on or near the thali depending on its size. In earlier times, food was served on plantain leaves or on a circular mat made by fastening dried leaves together with thin sticks like toothpicks and the liquid food was served in bowls made from dried leaves. This practice is still followed in the smaller towns and villages.

Generally speaking, all items of food such as breads, dals, curries, pickles and accompaniments such as raitas are served together, although rice and papadums may be offered separately. Sweets are not eaten daily but when served, they are usually eaten with the meal. Savouries, some of which can also be eaten as snacks, are also served with the meals although, like sweets, they are not eaten daily. No drinks are served except cold water and in some parts of India like Gujarat, salted buttermilk. Food is eaten with the fingers as knives and forks are just not appropriate for eating the Indian breads. The method of eating these is to tear off a portion of bread and use it to scoop some dal, curry or vegetable. The food is usually eaten with the right hand; and the left hand, which is kept clean, is used for drinking water and also for taking additional portions of the dishes.

The type of food and the manner of eating varies from region to region but generally speaking, a combination of a vegetable dish, curry or dal with bread and an accompaniment, followed if desired by a rice dish, would be fairly representative of a typical menu. Soups and sweets are optional. Boiled rice goes better with the spicier dals and curries. Similarly, in combining breads with curry, a good rule would be to use plain parathas, chapatis or puris with a spicy curry or dal and to serve natural yogurt with the spicier rotis and parathas. I have included a recipe for a sweet bread – such breads are commonly eaten at festivals in Western India. By way of guidance, I have suggested a few menus and you can follow these for making up your own combinations of dishes.

MENUS

VEGETABLE AND DAL SOUP (page 15)
MOGLAI POTATOES (page 34)
MASALA DAL (page 50)
POTATO ROTI (page 82)
CUCUMBER SALAD (page 74)
BOILED RICE (page 123)
PANEER AND COCONUT BALLS (page 114)

———————— * ————————

YOGURT SHORBA (page 14)
KHAMIRI PEA PURIS (page 83)
SPICY YOGURT (page 77)
MASALA KHICHADI WITH CURRY SAUCE (page 72)
NARANGI NI BASUNDI (page 120)

———————— * ————————

VEGETABLE AND RICE SOUP (page 15)
AUBERGINES IN CHILLI-GARLIC SAUCE (page 41)
SWEET & SOUR VEGETABLES WITH
CRISPY NOODLES (page 32)
MANCHURIAN VEGETABLES (page 32)
ORANGE SANDESH (page 119)

———————— * ————————

PANEER MUTTER KORMA (page 44)
BROAD BEAN CURRY (page 54)
KORMA RICE (page 69)
MOONG DAL TIKKAS (page 106)
PAPADUMS (page 77)
MALAI PUDAS (page 117)

Soups

Soups are optional extras in Indian meals as they do not form part of traditional menus. However, many Indian ingredients can be used to enliven vegetable soups: aromatic spices, hot or mild chillies, dals and yogurt all add interest to these simple dishes.

In this chapter the soups range from a refreshing and spicy Yogurt Shorba to an unusual Vegetable Soup with Crisp Vermicelli which is served with chillies in vinegar. There are filling soups, too, like Vegetable and Dal Soup or Vegetable and Rice Soup; served with parathas these are substantial enough to form a meal on their own.

When you plan to serve soup along with other dishes, then present it as a first course with papadums or chapatis. If the soup is to be served hot, it is important to make sure that it is steaming hot and not just lukewarm. Try to remember that the starter should tempt the appetite for the rest of the meal, so before you pour the soup into bowls taste it to make sure that the seasoning is just right and serve moderately sized portions which are not too filling.

Yogurt Shorba

Serves 4

450 ml/¾ pint natural yogurt
1 teaspoon plain flour
2 tablespoons milk
25 g/1 oz ghee
½ teaspoon cumin seeds
½ onion, chopped
2 green chillies, chopped

½ teaspoon grated fresh root ginger
salt to taste
2–4 teaspoons chopped tomatoes
2 tablespoons chopped cucumber
1 tablespoon chopped fresh
coriander leaves

1 Beat the yogurt, plain flour and milk together.

2 Melt the ghee and fry the cumin seeds in it for a few seconds. Add the onion, green chillies and ginger. Continue to fry for a few seconds.

3 Stir in the yogurt mixture and salt. Add the tomato and cucumber, heat until the mixture just boils, then remove from the heat. Serve immediately, sprinkled with the chopped coriander.

Lentil and Tomato Shorba

Serves 6

1 tablespoon oil or ghee
2 onions, sliced
2 cloves garlic, crushed
275 g/10 oz masoor dal, washed

1 kg/2 lb tomatoes, chopped
1.4 litres/2½ pints water
salt to taste
a little boiled rice to serve

1 Heat the oil or ghee in a saucepan. Add the onions and garlic and fry for 2 minutes. Add the dal and tomatoes, then continue to cook for 5–7 minutes.

2 Pour in the water and bring to the boil. Reduce the heat, cover the pan and simmer until the dal are soft. This should take about 30–40 minutes.

3 Allow the soup to cool slightly, then blend in a liquidiser until smooth and strain through a sieve. Return the soup to the saucepan. Heat through, taste and adjust the seasoning, then serve hot topped with a little boiled rice.

Vegetable and Dal Soup

Serves 4

3 large onions, chopped
4 large tomatoes, chopped
4 tablespoons moong dal
1.4 litres/2½ pints water

25 g/1 oz butter or 1 tablespoon oil
450 g/1 lb cabbage, shredded
450 g/1 lb spinach, chopped
salt and pepper to taste

1 Mix two-thirds of the chopped onions and half the chopped tomatoes with the dal in a saucepan. Pour in the water.

2 Bring to the boil, cover the pan and simmer for 1 hour. Blend in the liquidiser, then press through a sieve.

3 Melt the butter or heat the oil in a saucepan, add the remaining onion and fry for 1 minute. Add the cabbage and spinach and continue to fry for 1 minute. Pour in the sieved stock, bring to the boil and boil for 10 minutes.

4 Stir in the remaining chopped tomato, salt and pepper, bring to the boil, then cook for a few minutes. Serve hot with Parathas (page 80) or Potato Roti (page 82).

Vegetable and Rice Soup

Serves 4

50 g/2 oz butter
1 onion, chopped
1 quantity vegetable stock (page 122)
450 g/1 lb mixed vegetables

75 g/3 oz long-grain rice
450 ml/¾ pint milk
1 teaspoon lemon juice
salt and pepper to taste

1 Melt the butter in a saucepan, add the onion and cook for 1 minute. Add the stock, bring to the boil and boil the soup (uncovered) for 10 minutes.

2 Prepare the mixed vegetables according to their type and cut into bite-sized pieces. Add to the soup. Bring to the boil and cook for 20 minutes.

3 Add the rice and cook, uncovered, for a further 15 minutes. Stir in the milk, lemon juice, salt and pepper. Heat through, simmer gently for a few minutes, then serve.

Vegetable Soup with Crisp Vermicelli

Serves 6–8

3 tablespoons oil
100 g/4 oz cabbage, shredded
100 g/4 oz carrots, thinly sliced
½ cucumber, thinly sliced
1 tomato, sliced
a few lettuce leaves, shredded
½ teaspoon monosodium glutamate
1.4 litres/2½ pints vegetable stock
(page 122) or water

oil for deep frying
225 g/8 oz rice vermicelli, cooked
and drained
CHILLIES IN VINEGAR
2 red or green chillies
2 teaspoons white vinegar
soy sauce to serve

1 Heat the 3 tablespoons oil in a saucepan. Add the prepared vegetables and monosodium glutamate. Cook for 2–3 minutes, stirring frequently.

2 Add the stock or water and bring to the boil. Cook for 2–3 minutes.

3 Heat the oil for deep frying to 180 C/350 F, add the cooked vermicelli and fry until crisp and golden. Drain on absorbent kitchen paper, crumble the crisp noodles and add them to the soup.

4 Slice the red or green chillies into rings, discarding the stalks. Mix them with the vinegar.

5 Serve the soup immediately with soy sauce and the chillies in vinegar.

*Curried Vegetables in Tomato Sauce (page 23) with folded Chapatis
(page 80) and natural yogurt with chopped fresh coriander*

Sour and Hot Pepper Soup

Serves 6–8

2 red chillies
2 teaspoons white vinegar
2 tablespoons cornflour
$\frac{1}{4}$ teaspoon pepper
1–2 tablespoons soy sauce
1.4 litres/2$\frac{1}{2}$ pints vegetable stock
(page 122) or water
2 tablespoons oil

2 carrots, grated
100 g/4 oz white cabbage, shredded
1 onion, sliced
2 spring onions, chopped
$\frac{1}{4}$ teaspoon monosodium glutamate
salt to taste
chilli garlic sauce (page 41) and soy
sauce to serve

1 Slice the red chillies into rings, discarding the stalks. Mix them with the vinegar.

2 Blend the cornflour, pepper and soy sauce with a little of the stock or water until smooth. Add the remaining stock or water, pour into a saucepan and bring to the boil, stirring continuously.

3 Heat the oil in a frying pan, add the carrots, cabbage, sliced onion, spring onion and monosodium glutamate. Fry, stirring, over high heat for 3–4 minutes.

4 Add the fried vegetables to the cornflour mixture. Stir in the chillies in vinegar and salt. Bring back to the boil and cook for a few minutes.

5 Serve immediately with chilli garlic sauce and soy sauce.

Pages 20/21 *Clockwise from top left: Spiced Vegetables with Buttered Rice (page 27), Vegetable Ring (page 31), Coconut Curry Sauce (page 75) and Paneer Makhani (page 48)*

Vegetable Dishes

Vegetables, rice and dals together make up the main part of an Indian vegetarian diet. Prepared and cooked according to their type, a wide variety of vegetables are used in dishes which can be either hot or mild in flavour. Seasoned with specially selected whole or ground spices, simple vegetables are cooked in rich sauces for mouth-watering results. Alternatively, they may be chopped or mashed and moulded into vegetable koftas, then deep fried until crisp and golden.

In this chapter you will find that the recipes make full use of all these different cooking methods. Layered in baked dishes, shaped into patties or simply served whole and spiced – there are as many different ways of presenting vegetables as there are types to choose from.

And, when you're in a hurry, don't forget that frozen vegetables can also play a part in many of the recipes. Quick to prepare and cook, with an excellent flavour and colour, certain frozen vegetables – for example sweet corn and peas – can be used instead of, or as well as, fresh ones.

Vegetable Curry

Serves 4

1 kg/2 lb mixed vegetables – for
example, French beans, carrots, peas,
potatoes and cauliflower
2 onions, chopped
$\frac{1}{2}$ fresh coconut, grated
10 mild red chillies
10 teaspoons poppy seeds
7 cloves garlic
$\frac{1}{2}$ teaspoon turmeric

2.5-cm/1-in piece fresh root ginger,
grated
50 g/2 oz ghee
$\frac{1}{2}$ teaspoon garam masala (page 124)
300 ml/$\frac{1}{2}$ pint water
200 ml/7 fl oz natural yogurt
3 tablespoons single cream
1 teaspoon sugar
salt to taste

1 Prepare and cook the mixed vegetables according to their type, breaking
or cutting large ones into bite-sized pieces.

2 Grind the onions, coconut, chillies, poppy seeds, garlic, turmeric and
ginger to a paste.

3 Melt the ghee in a heavy-based saucepan, add the paste and cook for 3–4
minutes. Stir in the garam masala and cook for a further few minutes, then
add the vegetables and water. Bring to the boil and cook for a few minutes.

4 Stir in the yogurt, cream, sugar and salt, heat gently, then serve hot with
parathas (page 80).

Sabzi Panchmahal

Serves 4

2 tomatoes
3 onions
200 ml/7 fl oz water
1 kg/2 lb mixed vegetables – for
example, French beans, carrots,
potatoes and peas
1 tablespoon chopped cashew nuts
1 tablespoon poppy seeds
5 gloves garlic
2 teaspoons coriander seeds

1 teaspoon cumin seeds
7 red chillies
1-cm/$\frac{1}{2}$-in piece fresh root ginger,
grated
3 green cardamoms
50 g/2 oz ghee
salt to taste
4 tablespoons single cream
$\frac{1}{2}$ teaspoon sugar

1 Put the tomatoes in a bowl, pour in boiling water to cover and leave to
stand for 1 minute. Drain, peel and chop.

2 Roughly chop the onions and place them in a saucepan with half the water.
Bring to the boil, cover and simmer for about 15 minutes, or until the onions
are soft. Blend in a liquidiser until smooth.

3 Prepare the vegetables according to their type, cutting large ones into bite-
sized pieces, and cook lightly in boiling water. Drain and set aside.

4 Grind the cashew nuts, poppy seeds, garlic, coriander and cumin seeds, chillies, ginger and cardamoms to make a paste.

5 Melt the ghee in a heavy-based saucepan, add the paste and cook for 2–3 minutes. Stir in the chopped tomatoes and blended onion, then cook for a further 3–4 minutes.

6 Add the vegetables, salt and remaining water to the pan. Bring to the boil and cook at a simmer for a few minutes. Stir in the cream and sugar, make sure the sauce is well mixed and serve hot.

Curried Vegetables in Tomato Sauce

(Illustrated on page 17)

Serves 2

1.5 kg/3½ lb tomatoes	1 teaspoon mustard seeds
600 ml/1 pint water	1 teaspoon cumin seeds
4 potatoes	2 pinches asafoetida
225 g/8 oz okra	3 tablespoons gram flour
13–14 green chillies	100 g/4 oz French beans
2.5-cm/1-in piece fresh root ginger, grated	a few curry leaves
50 g/2 oz ghee	1 tablespoon garam masala (page 124)
	salt to taste

1 Quarter the tomatoes, place them in a saucepan and add the water. Bring to the boil, reduce the heat and simmer for 20 minutes.

2 Press the cooked tomatoes through a sieve, or blend them in a liquidiser, then press through a sieve. Cut the potatoes and okra into bite-sized pieces.

3 Grind ten of the chillies and ginger to make a paste. Split the remaining chillies open and reserve them for later use.

4 Melt the ghee in a heavy-based saucepan, add the mustard seeds, cumin seeds and asafoetida, then cook for a few minutes. Stir in the gram flour and cook, stirring, over gentle heat for 2–3 minutes.

5 Gradually pour in the blended tomatoes, stirring continuously. Add the prepared vegetables, French beans, curry leaves, remaining green chillies, garam masala, paste and salt.

6 Bring to the boil, reduce the heat and cover the pan. Simmer for 15–20 minutes or until the vegetables are cooked. Serve hot.

Overleaf *Clockwise from the left: Khamiri Pea Puris (page 83), Moglai Potatoes (page 34), Vegetable Rolls (page 101), tomatoes with chopped fresh coriander, cucumber with chilli powder and mango chutney*

Ceylonese Curry

Serves 4

2 fresh coconuts
1.15 litres/2 pints water
1 kg/2 lb mixed vegetables – for
example, carrots, peas and French
beans
$\frac{1}{4}$ teaspoon turmeric
1$\frac{1}{2}$ teaspoons ground coriander
1$\frac{1}{2}$ teaspoons ground cumin
2 teaspoon chilli powder
3 small cinnamon sticks
5 peppercorns
$\frac{1}{2}$ teaspoon ground fenugreek

2 onions, chopped
4 curry leaves
2 green chillies, slit
salt to taste
2 potatoes, boiled and finely
chopped
3 large tomatoes, finely chopped
SAMBOL
$\frac{1}{2}$ fresh coconut
1 onion, chopped
1 teaspoon chilli powder
1 teaspoon lemon juice

1 Pierce two of the eyes in the top of each coconut and drain off the coconut water. Crack open the nuts, remove and grate the flesh.

2 Place the grated coconut in a bowl with 300 ml/$\frac{1}{2}$ pint of the water. Leave to stand for 30 minutes, then gradually blend the mixture in a liquidiser and strain it through a fine sieve to obtain thick coconut milk.

3 Add the remaining water to the sieved coconut flesh and allow to stand for a further 30 minutes. Blend and sieve this mixture as before to obtain thin coconut milk.

4 Meanwhile, prepare the mixed vegetables, cutting any large ones into bite-sized pieces.

5 Pour the thin coconut milk into a saucepan. Add the vegetables, turmeric, coriander, cumin, chilli powder, cinnamon sticks, peppercorns, funugreek, chopped onions, curry leaves, slit chillies and salt. Bring to the boil, reduce the heat and cook until the vegetables are tender – about 15 minutes.

6 Stir in the potatoes, tomatoes and half the thick coconut milk. Cook for a few minutes before adding the last of the thick coconut milk.

7 To make the sambol, remove and grate the flesh from the coconut. Grind the grated coconut with the remaining ingredients and salt to taste to form a paste.

8 Serve the heated curry with plain cooked rice, cooked vermicelli or thin noodles and the sambol.

Spiced Vegetables with Buttered Rice

(Illustrated on pages 20/21)

Serves 6

2 dessert apples, cored
1 red or green pepper, trimmed
1 tomato
1 kg/2 lb mixed vegetables – for
example French beans, carrots, peas
and potatoes
1 onion, chopped
4 green chillies
2.5-cm/1-in piece fresh root ginger,
grated

25 g/1 oz ghee
1 teaspoon chilli powder
150 ml/$\frac{1}{4}$ pint tomato ketchup *or*
fresh tomato purée
150 ml/$\frac{1}{4}$ pint water
salt to taste
350 g/12 oz long-grain rice
50 g/2 oz butter
3 tablespoons single cream

1 Roughly chop the apples, pepper and tomato. Prepare and cook the mixed vegetables according to their type. Grind the onion, chillies and ginger to make a paste.

2 Melt the ghee in a saucepan, add the paste and cook for a few minutes. Add the apples, pepper, tomato and the chilli powder. Cook for 3–4 minutes. Stir in the vegetables, tomato ketchup or tomato purée, water and salt to taste, then cook for a few minutes, until heated through.

3 Cook the rice according to the instructions on page 123. Set aside and allow to cool. Melt the butter in a saucepan, add the rice and salt to taste. Toss to mix, then heat through over low heat.

4 Stir the cream into the spiced vegetables and serve with the buttered rice.

Spiced Vegetables

Serves 4–6

1 kg/2 lb mixed vegetables – for
example French beans, carrots,
courgettes and cauliflower
2 onions, chopped
6–7 green chillies
2.5-cm/1-in piece fresh root ginger,
grated

75 g/3 oz ghee
3 potatoes, boiled and cubed
2 tablespoons chopped fresh
coriander leaves
$\frac{1}{2}$ teaspoon garam masala (page 124)
1 teaspoon lemon juice
salt to taste

1 Prepare and cook the vegetables according to their type. Grind half the chopped onion to a paste with the chillies and ginger.

2 Melt the ghee in a saucepan, add the remaining onion and fry for 1 minute. Add the paste and continue to fry for 1 minute.

3 Add the mixed vegetables, potatoes, coriander, garam masala, lemon juice and salt. Cook, stirring, for a few minutes to heat through. Serve hot.

Baked Masala Vegetables

Serves 4–6

1 small cauliflower, lightly cooked
4 carrots, cooked
2 onions, chopped
3 green chillies
1-cm/½-in piece fresh root ginger,
grated
oil or ghee for deep frying
12 small new potatoes

50 g/2 oz butter
½ teaspoon chilli powder
100 g/4 oz peas, cooked
salt to taste
SAUCE
25 g/1 oz butter
25 g/1 oz plain flour
600 ml/1 pint milk

1 Cut the cauliflower into florets and cut the carrots into long strips. Grind half the chopped onion to a paste with the chillies and ginger.

2 Heat the oil or ghee for deep frying to 180 C/350 F, add the potatoes and cook until golden brown. Drain on absorbent kitchen paper and set aside.

3 Melt the butter in a saucepan and fry the remaining onion in it for a few minutes. Add the paste and fry for a further ½ minute. Stir in the chilli powder, cooked vegetables and salt to taste, then transfer the mixture to an ovenproof dish.

4 To make the sauce, melt the butter in a saucepan, stir in the flour and cook, stirring, for 1 minute. Gradually pour in the milk and bring to the boil, still stirring. Add salt to taste.

5 Pour the sauce over the vegetables and bake in a hot oven (230 C, 450 F, gas 8) for 20 minutes or until browned on top. Serve immediately.

Pea and Potato Patties (page 35) and Gado Gado (page 78)

Quick Baked Vegetables

Serves 4

450 g/1 lb mixed vegetables – for example, French beans, cauliflower, carrots, and peas
2 potatoes, lightly boiled
ghee for deep frying
1 aubergine, sliced
450 g/1 lb tomatoes
200 ml/7 fl oz water
50 g/2 oz butter

1 onion, chopped
1 tablespoon plain flour
$\frac{1}{2}$ teaspoon chilli powder
1 teaspoon chilli sauce (optional)
1–2 teaspoons sugar
1 teaspoon vinegar
salt to taste
350 g/12 oz paneer, chopped (page 122)
2 tablespoons single cream

1 Prepare and lightly cook the mixed vegetables according to their type. Slice the potatoes. Heat the ghee for deep frying to 180 C/350 F and cook the potatoes until lightly browned. Drain on absorbent kitchen paper. Deep fry the aubergine in the hot ghee.

2 Roughly chop the tomatoes and place them in a saucepan with the water. Cook gently for 15 minutes or until the tomatoes form a pulp. Press through a sieve and set aside.

3 Melt half the butter in a saucepan and fry the onion for 1 minute. Add the flour and fry for a further $\frac{1}{2}$ minute. Stir in the tomato pulp, chilli powder, chilli sauce (if used), sugar, vinegar and salt. Mix well. Add the mixed vegetables, 225 g/8 oz of the paneer and cream, then cook for a few minutes to heat through.

4 Arrange a layer of potato and aubergine slices in an ovenproof dish. Spread the vegetable mixture over, then layer the remaining potato and aubergine slices on top. Top with the reserved paneer.

5 Dot with the remaining butter and bake in a hot oven (230 C, 450 F, gas 8) for about 15 minutes. Serve immediately.

Note: Grated Cheddar cheese can be used instead of the paneer as a topping for this dish.

Vegetable Ring

(Illustrated on back cover and pages 20/21)

Serves 6

4 medium potatoes
salt to taste
about 450 g/1 lb mixed vegetables –
for example, French beans, carrots,
and peas
large bunch of fresh coriander
leaves, trimmed and chopped
6 green chillies
2.5-cm/1-in piece fresh root ginger,
grated
4 tablespoons grated fresh coconut

juice of 1 lemon
1 teaspoon sugar
100 g/4 oz cooked long-grain rice
225 g/8 oz frozen sweet corn, cooked
6 tablespoons oil
2 teaspoons mustard seeds
4 teaspoons sesame seeds
4 tablespoons chopped cashew nuts
1 tomato, sliced
1 green pepper, sliced
2 pinches asafoetida

1 Peel and quarter the potatoes, place them in a saucepan and cover with water. Add a little salt, bring to the boil, then reduce the heat and cover the pan. Simmer for 20 minutes until the potatoes are tender, then drain and mash them.

2 Prepare and cook the mixed vegetables according to their type and dice any large ones.

3 Meanwhile, grind the chopped coriander leaves with the chillies, ginger, coconut, lemon juice and sugar to make a paste. Add 1 teaspoon salt to the paste.

4 Combine the potatoes, mixed vegetables, rice and sweet corn. Add the paste, season with salt to taste and mix well.

5 Heat half the oil in a heavy-based frying pan, add half the mustard seeds and fry for 1 minute. Add half the sesame seeds and half the nuts and continue to fry for a few minutes.

6 Stir the fried ingredients into the vegetable mixture.

7 Arrange the tomato and pepper slices in the bottom of a well-greased 1.4-litre/2$\frac{1}{2}$-pint ring tin.

8 Spoon the vegetable mixture into the tin, pressing it down well. Cover with cooking foil and bake in a moderately hot oven (200 C, 400 F, gas 6) for about 40 minutes.

9 Heat the remaining oil in a frying pan, add the remaining mustard seeds and cook for 1 minute. Add the asafoetida, the remaining sesame seeds and nuts. Fry, stirring, for a few minutes.

10 Turn out the vegetable ring on to a hot serving dish. Pour over the fried mixture and serve hot with Coconut Curry Sauce (page 75).

Sweet and Sour Vegetables with Crispy Noodles

Serves 4

450 g/1 lb cabbage
225 g/8 oz cauliflower
1 large tomato
2 carrots
1 onion
$\frac{1}{4}$ teaspoon monosodium glutamate
salt to taste
1 (425-g/15-oz) can pineapple rings

450 g/1 lb chinese egg noodles
SAUCE
5 tablespoons white vinegar
150 ml/$\frac{1}{4}$ pint tomato ketchup
2 tablespoons sugar
1 tablespoon plain flour
3 tablespoons oil
oil for deep frying

1 Shred the cabbage and thinly slice the cauliflower, tomato, carrots and onion. Mix all the vegetables, add the monosodium glutamate and salt.

2 Drain the pineapple slices, reserving the syrup, and chop them into small pieces.

3 Cook the noodles in plenty of boiling salted water until tender – about 10 minutes. Drain and set aside.

4 Mix the ingredients for the sauce (except for the oil) until smooth, then add the reserved pineapple syrup. Cook, stirring continuously, over gentle heat until the sauce boils and becomes thick.

5 Heat the 3 tablespoons oil in a large frying pan. Add the vegetables and pineapple. Cook over high heat for 3–4 minutes, stirring frequently.

6 Heat the oil for deep frying to 180 C/350 F and cook the noodles in it, a few at a time, until crisp. Drain on absorbent kitchen paper, break up and arrange on a serving dish.

7 Put the vegetables on top of the noodles and pour the sauce over them. Serve immediately.

Manchurian Vegetables

Serves 4–6

450 g/1 lb cabbage, finely shredded
or grated
225 g/8 oz carrots, grated
1 onion, grated
2 tablespoons cornflour
5 tablespoons plain flour
3–4 cloves garlic, finely chopped
1 green chilli, chopped
salt to taste
2 pinches ground black pepper
$\frac{1}{4}$ teaspoon monosodium glutamate

oil for deep frying
SAUCE
2 tablespoons oil
1 tablespoon finely chopped garlic
1 tablespoon finely chopped green
chillies
4 tablespoons soy sauce
1 tablespoon cornflour
150 ml/$\frac{1}{4}$ pint water
pinch of monosodium glutamate

1 Mix the cabbage, carrots, onion, cornflour, flour, garlic, chopped chilli, salt, pepper and monosodium glutamate. Shape spoonfuls of the mixture into balls about the size of small eggs, then flatten them slightly.

2 Heat the oil for deep frying to 180 C/350 F and fry the vegetable balls a few at a time until golden brown. Drain on absorbent kitchen paper and keep hot.

3 To make the sauce, heat the oil, add the garlic with the chopped chillies and fry for a few seconds.

4 Mix the soy sauce and cornflour with little of the water. Add the remaining water and pour the mixture into the pan with the garlic and chillies. Bring to the boil, simmer for 1 minute, then add the monosodium glutamate and a little salt.

5 Arrange the vegetable balls on a serving dish, pour the hot sauce over and serve immediately.

Masala Potatoes with Peas

Serves 2

$\frac{1}{2}$ fresh coconut
600 ml/1 pint water
2 teaspoons coriander seeds
1 teaspoon cumin seeds
2 teaspoons poppy seeds
6–7 mild red chillies
2.5-cm/1-in piece fresh root ginger, grated
6 cloves garlic, crushed

1 large onion, chopped
50 g/2 oz ghee
2 tomatoes, chopped
225 g/8 oz peas
2 large potatoes, cut into cubes
salt to taste
$\frac{1}{2}$ teaspoon sugar
1 tablespoon chopped fresh coriander leaves

1 To make coconut milk, remove all the coconut from its shell and grate coarsely. Reserve 1 tablespoon of the grated coconut. Place the remainder in a bowl and add 450 ml/$\frac{3}{4}$ pint of the water, then allow to stand for about 30 minutes.

2 Grind the coriander, cumin and poppy seeds with the chillies, reserved coconut, ginger, garlic and onion to form a paste.

3 Melt the ghee in a saucepan, add the paste and fry for a few minutes. Add the chopped tomatoes and cook for 2 minutes. Stir in the peas and potatoes and continue to fry for a further 2 minutes.

4 Add 200 ml/7 fl oz of the coconut milk, the remaining water and salt. Bring just to the boil, reduce the heat and simmer, covered, until the vegetables are tender – about 20 minutes.

5 Stir in the remaining coconut milk and the sugar. Heat through, then sprinkle the chopped coriander on top and serve immediately with hot parathas (page 80).

Moglai Potatoes

(*Illustrated on pages 24/25*)

Serves 4

10–12 new potatoes or small old potatoes
4 cloves
2–3 teaspoons poppy seeds
2 green cardamoms
2 green chillies
1-cm/$\frac{1}{2}$-in piece fresh root ginger, grated
3 gloves garlic
150 ml/$\frac{1}{4}$ pint natural yogurt
salt to taste

50 g/2 oz ghee
2 onions, grated
1 teaspoon ground coriander
1 teaspoon ground cumin
1 teaspoon chilli powder
$\frac{1}{4}$ teaspoon turmeric
450 ml/$\frac{3}{4}$ pint water
100 g/4 oz peas
2 tablespoons single cream
$\frac{1}{2}$ teaspoon sugar

1 Scrub, scrape or peel the potatoes, then prick them thoroughly using a cocktail stick. Place the potatoes in a basin, cover with cold water and allow to soak for about 10 minutes.

2 Grind the cloves, poppy seeds, cardamoms, chillies, ginger and garlic to a paste.

3 Drain the potatoes, then mix them with the yogurt, paste and salt. Allow to stand for 1 hour.

4 Melt the ghee in a heavy-based saucepan and fry the grated onion in it for a few minutes. Add the coriander, cumin, chilli powder and turmeric. Continue to fry for 2–3 minutes.

5 Stir in the potato mixture and water, heat to simmering point and cook, uncovered, until the potatoes are tender. This should take about 15–20 minutes.

6 Add the peas, cream and sugar, stir well and cook for a few minutes until the peas are tender, then serve hot.

Note: If you like, you can first fry the potatoes in ghee until golden brown all over.

Pea and Potato Patties

(Illustrated on page 29)

Serves 4–6

BATTER
50 g/2 oz plain flour
salt to taste
200 ml/7 fl oz water
PATTIES
small bunch of fresh coriander
leaves, trimmed
3 green chillies, chopped
1 tablespoon grated fresh coconut
$\frac{1}{2}$ teaspoon sugar
$\frac{1}{2}$ teaspoon salt
225 g/8 oz peas, cooked
1 kg/2 lb potatoes, boiled, cooled and
grated

2 tablespoons cornflour
juice of $\frac{1}{2}$ lemon
a little plain flour
SAUCE
2 tomatoes
25 g/1 oz ghee
1 onion, grated
$\frac{1}{4}$–$\frac{1}{2}$ teaspoon chilli powder
2 tablespoons concentrated tomato
purée
200 ml/7 fl oz water

1 Make a thin batter by sifting the flour into a bowl with a little salt, gradually beating in the water until smooth. Allow to stand.

2 Grind the trimmed coriander leaves with two of the chillies, coconut, half the sugar and $\frac{1}{2}$ teaspoon salt to make a paste.

3 Mash the peas with the paste, remaining sugar and $\frac{1}{2}$ teaspoon salt.

4 Mix the potatoes with the cornflour, lemon juice, remaining chilli and salt to taste.

5 Take a spoonful of the potato mixture and knead it into a ball about the size of a small egg. Flatten the mixture in the palm of your hand to give a small patty.

6 Place a spoonful of the mashed peas in the middle of the patty, then bring the potato mixture up around it to form a ball. Flatten the ball to make a neat potato patty, enclosing the pea mixture, and lightly coat it with flour.

7 Place the tomatoes in a bowl, cover with boiling water and allow to stand for 1 minute. Drain, peel and finely chop.

8 Heat the ghee in a saucepan, add the onion and cook until golden brown. Stir in the tomato pulp, chilli powder and salt to taste, then add the tomato purée and water. Bring to the boil, cover and simmer steadily for 20 minutes.

9 Heat the oil for deep frying to 180 C/350 F. Dip the patties in the batter then deep fry them until crisp and golden. Drain on absorbent kitchen paper.

10 Place the halved cooked patties on a serving platter and pour the hot sauce over them. Serve immediately.

Green Peas Ambti

Serves 6

5 tablespoons oil
1 large onion, chopped
2 tablespoons grated coconut
2 teaspoons coriander seeds
3 cinnamon sticks
1 teaspoon cumin seeds
3 cloves
3 peppercorns
6 red chillies

6 cloves garlic
450 g/1 lb peas
300 ml/$\frac{1}{2}$ pint water
salt to taste
3–4 tablespoons tamarind water or 2
teaspoons tamarind paste
chopped fresh coriander leaves to
garnish

1 Heat 2 tablespoons of the oil in a frying pan and fry the onion with the coconut, coriander, cinnamon sticks, cumin seeds, cloves, peppercorns and chillies for at least 3–4 minutes. Grind all these fried ingredients together with the garlic to make a paste.

2 Heat the remaining oil in a saucepan, add the peas, paste, water and salt. Stir in the tamarind water or tamarind paste and bring to the boil. Reduce the heat and simmer for about 15 minutes or until the peas are cooked.

3 Serve hot garnished with the chopped fresh coriander.

Note: Tamarind water can be made by soaking 1 tablespoon chopped tamarind in 3–4 tablespoons water. Allow to stand for about 1 hour, then strain through a sieve.

Masala Corn with Peas

Serves 4

2 large tomatoes
2 teaspoons coriander seeds
1 teaspoon cumin seeds
2 cinnamon sticks
2 cloves
10–12 red chillies
2.5-cm/1-in piece fresh root ginger,
grated
5 cloves garlic
2 large onions, chopped

50 g/2 oz ghee
225 g/8 oz peas
225 g/8 oz frozen sweet corn
300 ml/$\frac{1}{2}$ pint water
$\frac{1}{2}$ teaspoon sugar
salt to taste
200 ml/7 fl oz milk
5 tablespoons natural yogurt
2 tablespoons ground poppy seeds

1 Put the tomatoes in a bowl and pour over enough boiling water to cover them. Allow to stand for 1 minute, then drain and peel them. Grate the tomatoes into a bowl.

2 Grind the coriander and cumin seeds with the cinnamon, cloves, chillies, ginger, garlic and chopped onions to make a paste.

3 Melt the ghee and fry the paste in it for 3–4 minutes. Add the grated tomatoes and cook for a few minutes.

4 Add the peas, corn, water, sugar and salt and continue to cook for a few minutes.

5 Mix the milk, yogurt and ground poppy seeds, then stir this mixture into the vegetables. Bring to the boil, boil for 5 minutes and serve hot.

Spicy Sweet Corn

(Illustrated on pages 52/53)

Serves 4–6

25 g/1 oz ghee or butter
1 onion, chopped
4 green chillies, chopped
450 g/1 lb sweet corn
salt to taste

150 ml/$\frac{1}{4}$ pint single cream
150 ml/$\frac{1}{4}$ pint natural yogurt
3 tablespoons chopped fresh
coriander leaves

1 Melt the ghee or butter in a saucepan and fry the onion in it for a few minutes until soft. Add the chillies and fry for a few seconds.

2 Stir in the sweet corn and salt to taste. Cook for a few minutes, stirring frequently until the corn is hot. Add the cream, yogurt and chopped coriander. Cook gently until hot, then serve immediately.

Corn Curry

Serves 4

1 fresh coconut
900 ml/1½ pints water
1 onion, chopped
large bunch of fresh coriander
leaves, trimmed
6 green chillies
7 cloves garlic
4 teaspoons poppy seeds
2.5-cm/1-in piece fresh root ginger

25 g/1 oz ghee
2 cinnamon sticks
2 cloves
2 green cardamoms
juice of ½ lemon
350 g/12 oz frozen sweet corn
salt to taste
lemon wedges to garnish

1 Pierce two of the eyes in the top of the coconut, then drain out the coconut water and reserve it for another use. Break open the nut with a hammer, remove and grate the flesh. Reserve 1 tablespoon of the grated coconut.

2 To make coconut milk, place the grated coconut in a bowl, pour in the water and allow to stand for about 30 minutes. Blend the coconut and water in a liquidiser, then strain through a sieve.

3 Grind the onion with the coriander leaves, chillies, garlic, poppy seeds, ginger and reserved coconut until the ingredients are reduced to a paste.

4 Melt the ghee in a heavy-based saucepan and fry the paste in it for 2 minutes. Add the cinnamon, cloves and cardamoms, continue to fry for a few minutes, then stir in the lemon juice.

5 Add the corn, coconut milk and salt, mix well and simmer for about 10 minutes, until the corn is cooked. Serve hot, with wedges of lemon to garnish. Squeeze the lemon juice over the curry before eating it.

Masala Corn

Serves 4

8–10 pickling onions
ghee for deep frying
10–12 small new potatoes
7 green chillies
2 onions, chopped
2.5-cm/1-in piece fresh root ginger,
grated
3 tablespoons oil

1 green or red pepper, chopped
1 tomato, chopped
1 teaspoon chilli powder
350 g/12 oz sweet corn, cooked
3 teaspoons vinegar
salt to taste
bunch of spring onions to garnish

1 Boil the pickling onions in salted water until tender.

2 Heat the ghee for deep frying to 180 C/350 F. Add the potatoes and cook until golden. Drain on absorbent kitchen paper.

3 Grind four of the chillies to a paste with half the chopped onion and the ginger.

4 Heat the oil in a saucepan and fry the remaining chopped onion for a few minutes. Add the paste and continue to fry for a few minutes.

5 Stir in the pepper, tomato and chilli powder and fry for at least 3–4 minutes. Chop the remaining chillies.

6 Add the corn, cooked onions, potatoes, vinegar, chopped chillies and salt to taste. Cook, stirring occasionally, until all the ingredients are heated.

7 Chop the spring onions and sprinkle over the masala. Serve immediately.

Masala Gobhi

(*Illustrated on pages 104/105*)

Serves 4

1 kg/2 lb cauliflower
ghee or oil for deep frying
3 large tomatoes, quartered
150 ml/$\frac{1}{4}$ pint water
50 g/2 oz ghee
3 large onions, grated
5 cloves garlic
2.5-cm/1-in piece fresh root ginger, grated
$\frac{1}{2}$ teaspoon garam masala (page 124)
2 teaspoons chilli powder

1 teaspoon ground coriander
1 teaspoon ground cumin
450 g/1 lb new, or small old, potatoes, boiled
100 g/4 oz peas
salt to taste
3 tablespoons single cream
$\frac{1}{2}$ teaspoon sugar
chopped fresh coriander leaves to garnish

1 Break the cauliflower into large florets. Heat the ghee or oil for deep frying to 180 C/350 F, add the cauliflower, a few florets at a time, and cook until golden. Drain on absorbent kitchen paper.

2 Place the tomatoes in a saucepan, add the water and bring to the boil. Cover the pan, reduce the heat and simmer for 5 minutes. Press through a sieve.

3 Melt the 50 g/2 oz ghee, add the grated onions and fry until lightly coloured. Meanwhile, grind the garlic and ginger together to make a paste.

4 Stir the paste, garam masala, chilli powder, coriander and cumin into the fried onions and continue to cook for 1 minute.

5 Add the cauliflower, potatoes, peas, salt to taste and tomato stock, then cook for about 5 minutes to reheat all the vegetables and cook the peas.

6 Finally, stir in the cream and sugar and serve immediately, sprinkled with the chopped coriander leaves.

Vegetable Kheema

Serves 4

3 large tomatoes
5 green chillies, chopped
6–7 cloves garlic
1-cm/$\frac{1}{2}$-in piece fresh root ginger, grated
3 cloves
3 green cardamoms
8–10 peppercorns
1 teaspoon cumin seeds
1$\frac{1}{2}$ teaspoons chilli powder
5–6 tablespoons oil

4 onions, finely chopped
1 kg/2 lb cauliflower, trimmed and coarsely grated
$\frac{1}{4}$ teaspoon turmeric
150 ml/$\frac{1}{4}$ pint water
100 g/4 oz paneer (page 122); crumbled or khoya (page 123)
salt to taste
1 tablespoon chopped fresh coriander leaves

1 Put the tomatoes in a bowl and cover with boiling water. Allow to stand for 1 minute, then peel and grate them into a pulp.

2 Grind the chillies with the garlic, ginger, cloves, cardamoms, peppercorns, cumin seeds and chilli powder to make a paste.

3 Heat the oil in a saucepan and fry the onions in it until golden in colour. Add the paste and continue to fry for 3–4 minutes.

4 Add the grated cauliflower, turmeric and water. Bring to the boil, reduce the heat, then cover and cook for 10–12 minutes.

5 Uncover the pan and continue to simmer, stirring continuously, for about 2–3 minutes.

6 Add the crumbled paneer or khoya to the pan and mix well. Finally, add the tomato pulp and salt. Cook until the oil floats – about 5 minutes.

7 Sprinkle the coriander over and serve hot with parathas (page 80).

Aubergines in Chilli-garlic Sauce

(Illustrated on pages 56/57)

Serves 4–6

3 long aubergines
3 spring onions
$\frac{1}{4}$ teaspoon monosodium glutamate
CHILLI-GARLIC SAUCE
200 ml/7 fl oz tomato ketchup or
fresh tomato purée
1 teaspoon chilli oil
4 teaspoons chilli sauce

$\frac{1}{2}$ teaspoon finely grated fresh root
ginger
1 clove garlic, crushed
1 teaspoon sugar
salt to taste
oil for deep frying
3 tablespoons oil

1 You can peel the aubergines if you like, then cut them lengthwise into eights. Chop the spring onions and mix them with the monosodium glutamate.

2 Mix all the ingredients for the chilli-garlic sauce and make sure they are thoroughly combined.

3 Heat the oil for deep frying, add the aubergines and cook until soft. Drain on absorbent kitchen paper.

4 Heat the 3 tablespoons oil in a large frying pan. Add the spring onion mixture and cook for 1 minute. Add the aubergines and pour in the chilli sauce.

5 Cook gently until the aubergines are hot, then serve immediately.

Note: To make chilli oil, chop 4–5 red chillies and add them to 5 tablespoons heated oil. Allow to cool, then leave to stand for at least 2 hours. Store in an airtight bottle.

Stuffed Pumpkin

Serves 8

1 medium pumpkin
salt to taste
100 g/4 oz French beans
100 g/4 oz carrots
4 tablespoons oil
$\frac{1}{2}$ teaspoon mustard seeds
225 g/8 oz peas
3 teaspoons chilli powder
about $\frac{1}{2}$ teaspoon turmeric

2 teaspoons ground coriander
2 teaspoons ground cumin
1 tablespoon chopped fresh
coriander leaves
1 tablespoon grated fresh coconut
2 onions, grated
2 tomatoes, finely chopped
200 ml/7 fl oz natural yogurt
200 ml/7 fl oz water

1 Lightly peel the pumpkin and cut in half. Scoop out the seeds from both portions and sprinkle salt on the inside. Finely chop the French beans and carrots.

2 Heat half the oil in a saucepan and fry the mustard seeds in it for $\frac{1}{2}$ minute.

3 Add the chopped vegetables, peas, half the chilli powder, $\frac{1}{4}$ teaspoon of the turmeric, 1 teaspoon each of the coriander and cumin and salt to taste. Cover and cook gently until the vegetables are soft – about 15–20 minutes.

4 Stir in the chopped coriander leaves and grated coconut. Stuff the pumpkin halves with this vegetable mixture and place them in a large ovenproof dish or roasting tin.

5 Heat the remaining oil in a small saucepan, add the grated onions and fry until they are lightly coloured. Add the remaining coriander, cumin, chilli powder and a pinch of turmeric, then fry for a further $\frac{1}{2}$ minute. Stir in the tomatoes and cook for 3–4 minutes. Stir in the yogurt and salt to taste. Cook gently for 1 minute, then pour in the water.

6 Pour the sauce over the pumpkin halves, cover loosely with cooking foil and cook in a moderately hot oven (200 C, 400 F, gas 6) for about 45 minutes or until the pumpkin is tender. Serve hot.

Bread Koftas in Pumpkin Curry

(Illustrated on pages 92/93)

Serves 4

KOFTAS
6 thick slices bread
5 tablespoons natural yogurt
3 tablespoons plain flour
1 tablespoon chopped fresh
coriander leaves
4 green chillies, chopped
2 pinches bicarbonate of soda
salt to taste
oil for deep frying
PUMPKIN CURRY
225 g/8 oz small new or old potatoes,
boiled
225 g/8 oz peeled pumpkin flesh

450 ml/$\frac{3}{4}$ pint water
2 large tomatoes
50 g/2 oz ghee
3 onions, grated
1 tablespoon chilli powder
1$\frac{1}{2}$ teaspoons ground coriander
1$\frac{1}{2}$ teaspoons ground cumin
$\frac{1}{4}$ teaspoon turmeric
2 teaspoons Punjabi garam masala
(page 124)
200 ml/7 fl oz natural yogurt
50 g/2 oz peas
salt to taste

1 First prepare the koftas. Remove the crusts from the bread slices, break them into pieces and place in a bowl. Pour the yogurt over the bread and leave to soak for 20 minutes.

2 Add the flour, chopped coriander, chillies, bicarbonate of soda and salt to taste. Mix the ingredients thoroughly with a wooden spoon. Shape small spoonfuls of the mixture into balls about the size of walnuts.

3 Heat the oil for deep frying to 180 C/350 F, then fry the koftas a few at a time until golden brown. Drain on absorbent kitchen paper. While the oil is hot, deep fry the potatoes for the pumpkin curry until golden brown. Drain on absorbent kitchen paper and set aside.

4 Cut the pumpkin into 2.5-cm/1-in cubes and place them in a saucepan. Add about three-quarters of the water and bring to the boil. Reduce the heat and simmer, covered, for about 30 minutes or until the pumpkin is tender. Cool slightly then blend in a liquidiser until smooth.

5 Put the tomatoes in a bowl, pour over boiling water to cover and allow to stand for 1 minute. Peel and grate the tomatoes so that they form a pulp.

6 Melt the ghee in a saucepan and fry the grated onions in it until light brown in colour. Add the chilli powder, coriander, cumin, turmeric and garam masala. Continue to fry for a few seconds.

7 Pour in the yogurt, pumpkin and tomato pulps, then add the remaining water and cook for a few minutes. Add the peas, fried potatoes and salt to taste, then cook gently until the peas are cooked and the potatoes are hot.

8 Add the koftas to the curry, bring to the boil so that the koftas are hot and serve immediately.

Paneer Mutter Korma

(Illustrated on page 81)

Serves 4

450 g/1 lb paneer (page 122)
ghee or oil for deep frying
1 tablespoon poppy seeds
1 tablespoon chopped cashew nuts
2 tablespoons milk
2.5-cm/1-in piece fresh root ginger, grated
5 cloves garlic
50 g/2 oz ghee
3 onions, grated
2 cinnamon sticks
2 bay leaves
2 cloves

1 teaspoon chilli powder
600 ml/1 pint water
4 tomatoes, chopped
200 ml/7 fl oz natural yogurt
1½ teaspoons freshly ground garam masala (page 124)
2 teaspoons freshly ground roasted cumin seeds
1 teaspoon ground coriander
100 g/4 oz peas
2 tablespoons single cream
1 teaspoon sugar
salt to taste

1 Cut half the paneer into cubes and crumble the remainder.

2 Heat the ghee or oil for deep frying to 180 C/350 F, then fry the paneer cubes until golden. Drain carefully on absorbent kitchen paper.

3 Place the poppy seeds and cashew nuts in a small basin and add the milk. Leave to soak for 30 minutes, then grind to a paste with the ginger and garlic.

4 Melt the 50 g/2 oz ghee and fry the grated onions in it until lightly coloured. Add the cinnamon, bay leaves and cloves, then fry for a few minutes. Stir in the chilli powder and half the water, then continue to cook for 1 minute.

5 Place the tomatoes in a saucepan with a little water. Bring to the boil, cook for a few minutes, then blend in a liquidiser and press through a sieve. Add to the onion mixture and bring to the boil.

6 Stir in the yogurt, then add the garam masala, ground cumin, coriander and the paste. Cook gently for a few minutes. Add the remaining water, peas and the fried paneer. Bring to the boil and boil for 2 minutes.

7 Finally, add the crumbled paneer, fresh cream, sugar and salt. Stir carefully, then serve hot.

Note: To roast cumin seeds, or other whole spices, place them in a heavy-based frying pan and cook over medium heat, stirring continuously, until the seeds pop and change colour. Remove the roasted seeds from the pan immediately so that they do not overcook and become bitter.

Baked Paneer Mutter

Serves 4

3 large tomatoes
6 cloves garlic
2.5-cm/1-in piece fresh root ginger,
grated
8 mild red chillies
1 tablespoon chopped cashew nuts
1 tablespoon poppy seeds
2 teaspoons coriander seeds
1 teaspoon cumin seeds
50 g/2 oz ghee

450 g/1 lb peas
salt to taste
1 tablespoon single cream
$\frac{1}{2}$ teaspoon sugar
25 g/1 oz butter
15 g/$\frac{1}{2}$ oz plain flour
300 ml/$\frac{1}{2}$ pint milk
225 g/8 oz paneer (page 122)
2 green chillies, chopped

1 Roughly chop the tomatoes and place them in a saucepan. Add 1 tablespoon water and cook until they form a pulp. Press through a sieve.

2 Grind the garlic, ginger, red chillies, cashew nuts, poppy, coriander and cumin seeds to make a paste.

3 Melt the ghee and fry the paste for 2–3 minutes. Add the tomato pulp, peas and salt, stir well, then cook for a few minutes. Add the cream and sugar.

4 Melt the butter in a saucepan, add the flour and cook, stirring, for a minute. Gradually pour in the milk, stirring continuously over low heat until the sauce boils and thickens.

5 Cut the paneer into cubes, mix the green chillies and salt to taste, then stir both into the sauce.

6 Spoon the pea mixture into a greased ovenproof dish and top with the paneer mixture. Bake in a hot oven (230 C, 450 F, gas 8) for 20 minutes, until browned on top. Serve immediately.

Baked Paneer with Chutney

Serves 4

450 g/1 lb paneer (page 122)
large bunch of fresh coriander
leaves, trimmed
4 green chillies
3 tablespoons grated fresh coconut

$\frac{3}{4}$ teaspoon sugar
juice of $\frac{1}{2}$ lemon
salt to taste
2 tablespoons thick natural yogurt

1 Cut the paneer into 1-cm/$\frac{1}{2}$-in cubes. Place them on cooking foil on a baking tray.

2 Grind the coriander, chillies, coconut, sugar, lemon juice and salt to taste to make a paste. Mix the yogurt into the paste and spread the mixture over the paneer cubes.

3 Wrap the foil around the paneer and bake in a moderately hot oven (200 C, 400 F, gas 6) for 15 minutes. Serve hot.

Note: Home-made paneer can be fried and baked without melting. The prepared cheese can be stored in the refrigerator for about a week but if you do not have the time to make paneer, then certain cream cheeses can also be cooked successfully. However, most soft cream cheeses melt when heated so use firm, full fat soft cheese, for example Philadelphia cheese.

Yogurt Kofta Curry

(Illustrated on pages 88/89)

Serves 4

KOFTAS
150 ml/¼ pint natural yogurt
75 g/3 oz gram flour
2 tablespoons chopped fresh
coriander leaves
6 green chillies, chopped
1 teaspoon cumin seeds
2 pinches bicarbonate of soda
salt to taste
PASTE
2 teaspoons coriander seeds
1 teaspoon cumin seeds
2 teaspoons poppy seeds
1 onion, chopped
4 cloves garlic

2.5-cm/1-in piece fresh root ginger,
grated
2 green chillies
1 tablespoon chopped fresh
coriander leaves
¼ teaspoon turmeric
SAUCE
2 large tomatoes
300 ml/½ pint water
50 g/2 oz ghee
5 tablespoons milk
salt to taste
2 tablespoons single cream
½ teaspoon sugar
oil or ghee for deep frying

1 Mix all the ingredients for the koftas to make a thick batter.

2 Grind the coriander, cumin and poppy seeds with the onion, garlic, ginger, chillies, chopped coriander and turmeric to make a paste.

3 Roughly chop the tomatoes for the sauce and place them in a small saucepan with about three-quarters of the water. Bring to the boil, then reduce the heat and simmer for 15 minutes. Press through a sieve or blend the tomatoes and water in a liquidiser, then press through a sieve.

4 Melt the 50 g/2 oz ghee in a saucepan. Add the paste and cook for 3–4 minutes, stirring frequently to prevent it sticking to the pan.

5 Stir in the blended tomatoes, milk, salt and remaining water. Bring to the boil and boil steadily for 10 minutes.

6 Meanwhile, heat the oil or ghee for deep frying to 180 C/350 F. Drop spoonfuls of the kofta mixture into the hot oil, then fry until golden brown. Drain carefully on absorbent kitchen paper.

7 Stir the cream into the sauce and add the sugar. Carefully add the koftas and serve immediately with plain cooked rice or parathas (page 80).

Paneer Makhani

(Illustrated on pages 20/21)

Serves 2

225 g/8 oz paneer (page 122)
ghee or oil for deep frying
2 tablespoons natural yogurt
3 large tomatoes
75 g/3 oz ghee
3 onions, grated
1 teaspoon garam masala (page 124)
1 teaspoon ground coriander

1 teaspoon ground cumin
1½ teaspoons chilli powder
¼ teaspoon turmeric
salt to taste
200 ml/7 fl oz water
150 ml/¼ pint single cream
15 g/½ oz butter
chopped fresh coriander leaves to
garnish

1 Cut the paneer into fingers. Heat the ghee or oil for deep frying to 180 C/350 F, then add the paneer fingers, a few at a time, and cook until golden.

2 Carefully drain the fried paneer on absorbent kitchen paper, then transfer them to a plate and pour the yogurt over the fingers.

3 Place the tomatoes in a bowl, pour over boiling water to cover and allow to stand for 1 minute. Drain and peel the tomatoes, then chop them finely.

4 Melt the 75 g/3 oz ghee and fry the onions in it until lightly coloured. Add the garam masala, coriander, cumin, chilli powder, turmeric and salt. Fry for 1 minute. Stir in the chopped tomatoes, and continue to fry for at least 5 minutes or until the ghee floats.

5 Pour in the water, bring to the boil, then reduce the heat and add the cream. Cook for a few minutes, then stir in the butter. Add the fried paneer and yogurt, heat through and garnish with the chopped coriander. Serve hot.

Dal Dishes

Dals are split pulses: dried beans and lentils. This chapter contains recipes for the whole pulses as well as the split dals. Rich in protein, these ingredients are most important in a vegetarian diet; served with rice and bread they make a complete and nourishing meal.

Dried beans should be stored in airtight containers but, although they do have a remarkably long shelf life, remember that you cannot store them forever. Before you cook the pulses, carefully sort through them and discard any that are discoloured, at the same time throw away any small bits of grit or dirt which may be mixed up with them. To clean the dals or beans, rinse them under running water, then cover them with cold water and leave to soak overnight. Next day, drain the beans and throw away any that are wrinkled and have not absorbed the water.

When cooked, you will find that the mild flavour of the pulses is readily influenced by the addition of spices and other well-flavoured ingredients in a variety of delicious dishes.

Masala Dal

(Illustrated on page 100)

Serves 4

100 g/4 oz moong dal
100 g/4 oz masoor dal
100 g/4 oz urad dal
100 g/4 oz toovar dal
1.15 litres/2 pints water
2 teaspoons coriander seeds
1 teaspoon cumin seeds
8 mild red chillies
$\frac{1}{4}$ teaspoon turmeric
3 cinnamon sticks
3 peppercorns

3 cloves
5 cloves garlic, crushed
2.5-cm/1-in piece fresh root ginger, grated
1 tablespoon chopped fresh coriander leaves
50 g/2 oz ghee
3 onions, grated
2 tomatoes, chopped
salt to taste
fresh coriander leaves to garnish

1 Place all the dals in a colander and wash them thoroughly under running water. Place the dals in a saucepan. Add the water and bring to the boil. Cover the pan, reduce the heat and cook for about 50 minutes, or until the water has been absorbed.

2 Meanwhile, grind the coriander and cumin seeds with the chillies, turmeric, cinnamon, peppercorns, cloves, garlic, ginger and chopped coriander leaves to form a paste.

3 Melt the ghee, add the grated onions and fry until lightly coloured. Stir in the paste and continue to fry for 3–4 minutes. Add the chopped tomatoes and cook for a further 3–4 minutes.

4 Finally, add the cooked dals and salt, stirring to combine all the ingredients. Cook for 5–7 minutes, then serve hot garnished with coriander leaves.

Rajma Curry

(*Illustrated on page 85*)

Serves 4–6

350 g/12 oz red kidney beans
7 cloves of garlic
7 green chillies, chopped
2.5-cm/1-in piece fresh root ginger,
grated
50 g/2 oz ghee
2 onions, grated

1 teaspoon chilli powder
450 g/1 lb tomatoes
450 ml/¾ pint water
2 teaspoons sugar
salt to taste
2 tablespoons chopped fresh
coriander leaves (optional)

1 Soak the red kidney beans overnight.

2 Drain the beans, put them in a saucepan with enough water to come at least 2.5 cm/1 in over the top of the beans and bring to the boil. *Boil for 3 minutes*, then reduce the heat, cover the pan and simmer for about 45 minutes, until the beans are tender. Check that the water level has not fallen below the beans during cooking and add more boiling water if necessary.

3 Meanwhile, grind the garlic, chillies and ginger to a paste.

4 Melt the ghee, add the grated onions and fry for 2–3 minutes. Add the paste and chilli powder and continue to fry for 1 minute. Add the drained cooked beans.

5 Cut the tomatoes into quarters and place them in a saucepan with the water. Bring to the boil, reduce the heat and simmer for 5 minutes. Press through a sieve to give a tomato stock.

6 Add the tomato stock to the beans with the sugar and salt. Cook, stirring, for a few minutes and serve hot, sprinkled with chopped coriander if you like.

Overleaf *From the left: Spicy Sweet Corn (page 37), Bean Hotpot (page 55), Cabbage Wadas (page 107) and Papadums (page 77)*

Broad Bean Curry

Serves 4–6

450 g/1 lb dried broad beans
4 tomatoes
150 ml/¼ pint water
2 onions
5–6 cloves garlic
6 mild red chillies
3 teaspoons coriander seeds

1 teaspoon cumin seeds
2 teaspoons poppy seeds
4–5 peppercorns
4–5 cloves
2–3 cinnamon sticks
25 g/1 oz ghee
salt to taste

1 Soak the beans overnight.

2 Place the drained beans in a saucepan and pour in enough water to come about 2.5 cm/1 in over the top of the beans. Bring to the boil, reduce the heat and cover the pan, then simmer for about 45 minutes or until the beans are tender.

3 Cut the tomatoes into quarters and place them in a saucepan with the water. Bring to the boil, reduce the heat and simmer for 5 minutes. Press through a sieve.

4 Roast the unpeeled onions over a gas flame or under a hot grill until black. Cool slightly, then remove the peel and grind the flesh to a paste with all the remaining ingredients except for the ghee and salt.

5 Melt the ghee in a heavy-based saucepan and fry the paste in it for 3–4 minutes. Add the drained, cooked beans, tomato stock and salt. Stir well, then cook for a few minutes. Serve hot with parathas (page 80).

Bean Hotpot

(Illustrated on back cover and pages 52/53)

Serves 4

100 g/4 oz dried broad beans
100 g/4 oz red kidney beans
100 g/4 oz black beans
1 kg/2 lb tomatoes
1 tablespoon ghee
1 onion, chopped
1 teaspoon chilli powder
2–3 teaspoons sugar
salt to taste

5–6 green chillies
2 thick slices bread
1 tablespoon chopped cashew nuts
or peanuts
1 tablespoon chopped fresh
coriander leaves
1 teaspoon lemon juice
4 potatoes, boiled and mashed
oil for deep frying

1 Soak all the beans together overnight. Drain and place them in a saucepan. Add enough cold water to come about 5 cm/2 in over the top of the beans. Bring to the boil, *boil for 3 minutes*, then reduce the heat and cover the pan. Simmer for about $1\frac{1}{2}$ hours or until the beans are tender.

2 Cut the tomatoes into quarters and place them in a saucepan. Add 2 tablespoons water and cook gently until the tomatoes are soft and pulpy – about 20 minutes. When cooked, press through a sieve.

3 Melt the ghee in a saucepan and fry the onion in it for 1 minute. Add the tomato pulp, chilli powder, sugar and salt to taste, and the drained beans. Split two of the chillies and add them to the pan. Bring to the boil and cook for about 10–15 minutes.

4 Remove the crusts from the bread, then quickly dip the slices in water. Squeeze out and crumble the bread. Mix the bread with the nuts, chopped coriander and lemon juice.

5 Chop the remaining chillies and add them to the mashed potatoes with the bread mixture. Make sure the ingredients are thoroughly combined and add salt to taste.

6 Shape the mixture into small balls about the size of walnuts. Heat the oil for deep frying to 180 C/350 F, then fry the potato balls until golden. Drain on absorbent kitchen paper.

7 Add the potato balls to the bean mixture and serve immediately.

Overleaf *From the left: Aubergines in Chilli-garlic Sauce (page 41), Green Peas Renedy (page 102) and Fruit and Vegetable Raita (page 76)*

Falafal

(Illustrated on page 61)

Serves 6

350 g/12 oz chick peas
4 green chillies, roughly chopped
$\frac{1}{2}$ teaspoon bicarbonate of soda
1 tablespoon chopped fresh
coriander leaves
salt to taste
oil for deep frying
HOT SAUCE
2 large tomatoes
10–12 red chillies, roughly chopped
5 cloves garlic
$\frac{1}{2}$ teaspoon lemon juice
salt to taste

SESAME SAUCE
2 tablespoons roasted sesame seeds
2 green chillies
4 tablespoons natural yogurt
$\frac{1}{2}$ teaspoon sugar
$\frac{1}{2}$ teaspoon mustard powder
SALAD
3 tomatoes, chopped
3 spring onions, chopped
225 g/8 oz white cabbage, shredded
salt to taste
12 pieces pitta bread to serve

1 Soak the chick peas overnight in cold water to cover.

2 Drain and grind the chick peas. Reserve 2 tablespoons of the ground chick peas. Grind the green chillies with the last batch of chick peas and mix in a large bowl with the bicarbonate of soda.

3 Add the chopped coriander and salt, then knead spoonfuls of the mixture into small balls about the size of walnuts.

4 Heat the oil for deep frying to 180 C/350 F and cook the chick pea balls a few at a time until golden brown. Drain on absorbent kitchen paper and set aside.

5 To make the hot sauce, start by peeling the tomatoes: place them in a bowl, cover with boiling water and allow to stand for 1 minute. Drain, peel and chop the tomatoes.

6 Mix the tomatoes with the chillies, garlic, lemon juice and salt. Blend these ingredients together in a liquidiser, adding a little water if necessary.

7 Place all the ingredients for the sesame sauce in a liquidiser and add the reserved ground chick peas. Blend until smooth, adding a little water if necessary.

8 Mix the ingredients for the salad and season lightly with salt. Slit the pieces of pitta bread and place a little salad in each. Top with chick pea balls, hot sauce and sesame sauce, then more salad. Serve two pieces of stuffed pitta per person for a filling meal.

Rice Dishes

Rice must be one of the most versatile ingredients and is used in cooking all over the world. Carefully spiced and flavoured, the rice is cooked to perfection in the dishes in this chapter – each grain is fluffy yet whole. Basmati rice offers the best flavour in cooking but other long-grain varieties can be used just as well. Pullaos, kormas and baked dishes are included; some are suitable for serving as a light meal on their own, while others make ideal accompaniments.

Mixed with dals, rice goes to make khichadi, a satisfying combination of two main ingredients which complement each other perfectly. Curries are also included with some of these rice dishes, as are vegetables and other flavouring ingredients like coconut. In fact, there is a rice dish suitable for every meal.

Bohri Khichadi

Serves 6

350 g/12 oz long-grain rice
225 g/8 oz toovar dal
salt to taste
a few saffron strands (optional)
5 red chillies
2 green chillies
2 small onions, chopped
4 cloves garlic

$1\frac{1}{2}$ teaspoons cumin seeds
3 large onions
ghee or oil for deep frying
75 g/3 oz ghee
1 teaspoon garam masala (page 124)
200 ml/7 fl oz natural yogurt
1 teaspoon sugar

1 Cook the rice according to the instructions on page 123 and allow to cool. Cook the dal according to the instructions on page 123. Cool.

2 To make the khichadi, mix the cooked rice and dal, adding salt to taste.

3 Place the saffron in a small bowl and add a little water. Stand the basin over hot water and rub the saffron until it dissolves. Add this saffron liquid to the khichadi.

4 Grind the red chillies with the green chillies, chopped small onions, garlic and cumin seeds to make a paste. Chop one of the large onions and slice the remaining onions.

5 Heat the ghee or oil for deep frying to 180 C/350 F, add the sliced onions, separated into rings, and cook until golden. Drain on absorbent kitchen paper and set aside.

6 Melt just over half the 75 g/3 oz ghee in a small saucepan. Add the chopped onion and fry for 1 minute. Add the paste and fry for a further 2 minutes. Stir in the garam masala and cook for a few seconds.

7 Remove the pan from the heat. Pour in the yogurt, sugar and salt to taste.

8 Use the remaining ghee to thoroughly grease an ovenproof dish. Place half the fried onion rings in the dish, spread half the khichadi over them and then pour the yogurt mixture over.

9 Mix the remaining onions with the second portion of khichadi and spread this over the yogurt. Cover with cooking foil and bake in a hot oven (230 C, 450 F, gas 8) for 15 minutes. Serve immediately.

From the top: Falafal (page 58) and Moong Dal Pudas (page 106)

Three-in-one Rice

(Illustrated on pages 92/93)

Serves 6–8

450 g/1 lb long-grain rice
salt to taste
ORANGE RICE
2–3 tomatoes
25 g/1 oz ghee
1 onion, chopped
2 carrots, grated
1 teaspoon sugar
2 green chillies, chopped
salt to taste
WHITE RICE
25 g/1 oz ghee
$\frac{1}{2}$ teaspoon black cumin seeds
2 green chillies, chopped
100 g/4 oz paneer (page 122), chopped

salt to taste
GREEN RICE
large bunch of fresh coriander
leaves, trimmed
4 green chillies
4 cloves garlic
2.5-cm/1-in piece fresh root ginger, grated
juice of $\frac{1}{2}$ lemon
25 g/1 oz ghee
1 onion, chopped
100 g/4 oz peas, cooked
salt to taste

1 Cook the rice according to the instructions on page 123, adding salt to taste. Drain (if necessary) and cool. Each grain of cooked rice should be separate.

2 Start by preparing the orange rice. Cut the tomatoes into quarters and place them in a saucepan. Add 2 tablespoons water and bring to the boil. Reduce the heat and cook for 10–15 minutes. Press the cooked tomatoes through a sieve to make a pulp.

3 Melt the ghee in a saucepan, add the onion and fry for 1 minute. Add the carrots and fry for a further 1 minute.

4 Pour in the tomato pulp, add the sugar, chillies and salt to taste. Cook for 2 minutes, then stir in one-third of the cooked rice. Mix well.

5 In a saucepan, melt the ghee for the white rice. Add the black cumin seeds and cook for a few seconds.

6 Stir in half the remaining rice, chillies and paneer. Add salt to taste and mix well.

7 To make the green rice, start by preparing a paste. Grind the coriander leaves, chillies, garlic, ginger and lemon juice together until fairly smooth.

8 Melt the ghee in a saucepan, add the onion and fry for 1 minute. Add the paste and continue to cook for a further 2 minutes. Stir in the remaining rice and peas, add salt to taste and mix well.

9 Layer the three rice combinations in a greased soufflé dish or firm-based cake tin. Cover closely with cooking foil and stand the container in a large saucepan.

10 Pour enough boiling water into the saucepan to come halfway up the side of the dish or tin. Stand the saucepan over medium heat. Cover the pan and steam the rice dish for 15 minutes.

11 To serve, invert the container on to a serving dish and serve immediately.

Paneer Mutter Pullao

(Illustrated on page 64)

Serves 6

350 g/12 oz long-grain rice
salt to taste
100 g/4 oz ghee
$\frac{1}{2}$ teaspoon black cumin seeds
2 cinnamon sticks
2 cloves
ghee or oil for deep frying
225 g/8 oz cauliflower florets
225 g/8 oz paneer (page 122), cut into cubes
100 g/4 oz peas
PASTE
1 onion, chopped
1 tomato, chopped
4 cloves garlic

7 red chillies
1-cm/$\frac{1}{2}$-in piece fresh root ginger, grated
3 teaspoons poppy seeds
2 teaspoons coriander seeds
1 teaspoon cumin seeds
3 green cardamoms
3 cloves
3 small cinnamon sticks
$\frac{1}{4}$ teaspoon turmeric
1 teaspoon salt
GARNISH
a few roasted cashew nuts
chopped fresh coriander leaves

1 Cook the rice according to the instructions on page 123, adding salt to taste, and allow to cool.

2 Melt half the ghee in a saucepan and add the black cumin seeds, cinnamon and cloves. Fry for $\frac{1}{2}$ minute. Add the cooked rice and salt to taste.

3 Heat the ghee or oil for deep frying to 180 C/350F, add the cauliflower florets and cook until golden. Drain on absorbent kitchen paper. Cook the paneer in the ghee, then drain carefully. Cook the peas.

4 Grind all the ingredients for the paste until fairly smooth.

5 Heat the remaining ghee in a saucepan and fry the paste for 3 minutes. Add the peas, cauliflower and paneer and mix well. Stir in the rice and mix well, then cook over very low heat for 10 minutes, or until the ingredients are hot.

6 Serve immediately, garnished with the cashew nuts and chopped coriander.

Pullao with Vegetables and Dal

Serves 6

350 g/12 oz long-grain rice
salt to taste
225 g/8 oz toovar dal
$\frac{1}{4}$ teaspoon saffron strands
225 g/8 oz mixed vegetables – for
example, French beans, carrots and
peas
3 large onions
2 tablespoons grated fresh coconut
8 mild red chillies

2.5-cm/1-in piece fresh root ginger,
grated
4 cloves garlic
3 teaspoons poppy seeds
3 green cardamoms
2 teaspoons coriander seeds
1 teaspoon cumin seeds
50 g/2 oz ghee
300 ml/$\frac{1}{2}$ pint natural yogurt
1 teaspoon sugar

1 Cook the rice according to the instructions on page 123, adding salt to taste, and allow to cool.

2 Place the toovar dal in a saucepan and add enough water to cover by at least 2.5 cm/1 in. Add salt to taste, bring to the boil, then reduce the heat and simmer for about 20 minutes, or until the dal are tender. Drain and cool.

3 Place the saffron in a small basin, add a little water – about 1 teaspoon – and stand the basin over hot water. Rub the saffron until it dissolves.

4 Prepare the mixed vegetables according to their type, cutting any large ones into bite-sized pieces, and cook in boiling salted water until tender. Chop one of the onions and slice the other two.

5 Grind the chopped onion, coconut, chillies, ginger, garlic, poppy seeds, cardamoms, coriander and cumin seeds to make a paste.

6 Melt the ghee in a frying pan. Add the sliced onions and fry them until lightly browned. Remove from the pan and set aside.

7 Add the paste to the ghee remaining in the pan and fry for 3–4 minutes. Remove the pan from the heat and stir in the yogurt, sugar and salt to taste.

8 Mix the cooked rice and dal with the vegetables, half the fried onion slices, saffron liquid and salt to taste.

9 Grease a straight-sided ovenproof dish (for example a soufflé dish). Layer the rice and vegetable mixture in the dish with the yogurt mixture. Top with the remaining sliced onions and cover with cooking foil.

10 Bake in a hot oven (230 C, 450 F, gas 8) for 20 minutes. Serve hot.

Paneer Mutter Pullao (page 63) and Semolina Pancakes (page 96)

Kashmiri Pullao

Serves 6

25 g/1 oz ghee
½ teaspoon black cumin seeds
2 cinnamon sticks
2 cloves
2 green cardamoms
2 bay leaves
350 g/12 oz long-grain rice

300 ml/½ pint milk
150 ml/¼ pint single cream
1 teaspoon sugar
salt to taste
450 ml/¾ pint water
1 (410-g/14½-oz) can fruit cocktail in
natural juice (drained)

1 Melt the ghee in a saucepan, add the cumin seeds and fry for a few minutes. Add the cinnamon, cloves, cardamoms and bay leaves. Stir in the uncooked rice and fry, without adding water, for 2–3 minutes.

2 Add the milk, cream, sugar, salt to taste and the water. Bring to the boil, then reduce the heat so that the rice simmers gently. When the rice is almost cooked, cover the pan and continue to cook very gently until all the water is absorbed.

3 Transfer the rice to a serving dish and toss in the fruit. Serve immediately, with curry sauce or with any vegetable curry.

Moglai Pullao

Serves 4

225 g/8 oz long-grain rice
salt to taste
450 g/1 lb mixed vegetables – for
example, carrots, peas and French
beans
75 g/3 oz ghee
½ teaspoon black cumin seeds
2 small cinnamon sticks
5 green cardamoms
3 cloves garlic

3 green chillies
1 tablespoon poppy seeds
5 cashew nuts
1½ teaspoons coriander seeds
1-cm/½-in piece fresh root ginger,
grated
150 ml/¼ pint natural yogurt
1 teaspoon sugar
1 onion, sliced

1 Cook the rice according to the instructions on page 123, adding salt to taste. Allow to cool. Prepare and cook the vegetables according to their type, cutting any large ones into bite-sized pieces.

2 Heat a quarter of the ghee, add the cumin seeds and fry for a few minutes. Add the cinnamon and two of the cardamoms and fry for a few seconds. Stir in the rice and salt to taste.

3 Grind the garlic, chillies, poppy seeds and remaining cardamoms with the cashew nuts, coriander seeds and ginger to make a paste.

4 Melt half the remaining ghee in a saucepan and fry the paste in it for a few minutes. Remove from the heat, add the yogurt, sugar and salt. Melt the remaining ghee in a frying pan and fry the onion for 1 minute.

5 Spread half the rice in the base of an ovenproof dish. Top the rice first with the yogurt mixture, then the vegetables and fried onion. Finally, spread the remaining rice on top.

6 Cover with cooking foil and bake in a hot oven (230 C, 450 F, gas 8) for 20 minutes. Serve immediately.

Saffron Pullao

(Illustrated on page 81)

Serves 6

450 g/1 lb long-grain rice	7 cloves garlic
salt to taste	50 g/2 oz ghee
a few saffron strands	3 onions, chopped
1 tablespoon milk	2 teaspoons chilli powder
225 g/8 oz French beans	$\frac{1}{2}$ teaspoon turmeric
225 g/8 oz carrots	$\frac{1}{2}$ teaspoon garam masala (page 124)
225 g/8 oz potatoes	2 tablespoons ground coriander
225 g/8 oz peas	2 tablespoons ground cumin
2.5-cm/1-in piece fresh root ginger, grated	3 tomatoes, chopped

1 Cook the rice according to the instructions on page 123, adding salt to taste, and allow to cool.

2 Place the saffron in a small basin, add the milk and stand the bowl over hot water. Rub the saffron until it dissolves, then stir into the rice and mix well.

3 Cut the French beans, carrots and potatoes into bite-sized pieces. Cook them in boiling salted water until tender. Cook the peas in the same way. Drain and set aside.

4 Grind the ginger with the garlic to make a paste.

5 Melt the ghee in a saucepan and fry the onions in it until they are light brown in colour. Add the paste and fry for 1 minute. Stir in the chilli powder, turmeric, garam masala, ground coriander and cumin. Add the tomatoes and cook for a further 2–3 minutes. Add the vegetables and salt to taste, then mix well.

6 Layer the rice and vegetables alternately in an ovenproof dish beginning and ending with rice. Cover with cooking foil and bake in a moderately hot oven (200 C, 400 F, gas 6) for 30 minutes. Serve hot.

Fruit and Vegetable Pullao

Serves 6

8–10 dried apricots
225 g/8 oz paneer (page 122)
3 tablespoons plain flour
pinch of bicarbonate of soda
salt to taste
2 green chillies, chopped
2 tablespoons chopped fresh
coriander leaves
ghee for deep frying
225 g/8 oz long-grain rice
100 g/4 oz ghee
$\frac{1}{2}$ teaspoon black cumin seeds
2 cinnamon sticks
2 cloves
2 green cardamoms
100 g/4 oz peas
a few saffron strands

a little milk
300 ml/$\frac{1}{2}$ pint natural yogurt
$\frac{1}{2}$ teaspoon sugar
PASTE
1 large onion, chopped
3 tablespoons grated fresh coconut
5 cloves garlic
2 teaspoons coriander seeds
1 teaspoon cumin seeds
2 cinnamon sticks
3 cloves
3 green cardamoms
2 teaspoons poppy seeds
7–8 red chillies
2.5-cm/1-in piece fresh root ginger,
grated

1 Cut the apricots into small pieces and soak in cold water to cover for 1 hour. Drain.

2 Mix the paneer, flour and bicarbonate of soda with salt to taste, the chillies and chopped coriander leaves.

3 Heat the ghee for deep frying to 180 C/350 F. Form spoonfuls of the paneer mixture into balls about the size of walnuts and deep fry until golden brown. Drain these koftas and set aside.

4 Cook the rice according to the instructions on page 123, adding salt to taste, and allow to cool.

5 Melt half the 100 g/4 oz ghee in a saucepan. Add the black cumin seeds, cinnamon, cloves and cardamoms and fry for $\frac{1}{2}$ minute. Add the rice, peas and salt to taste. Cook for a few minutes.

6 Warm the saffron with a little milk in a small basin over hot water. Rub in the saffron until it dissolves. Add to the rice. Stir in the apricot pieces.

7 Mix the yogurt with the sugar and add salt to taste.

8 Grind together all the ingredients for the paste until smooth.

9 Heat the remaining ghee in a small saucepan, add the paste and fry for 3–4 minutes. Remove the pan from the heat and stir in the seasoned yogurt.

10 Add the paneer koftas to the rice and spread one-third of the mixture in a greased ovenproof dish. Spoon half the yogurt sauce over. Arrange half the remaining rice over the sauce.

11 Top first with the remaining sauce, then with the last of the rice. Cover with the cooking foil and bake in a hot oven (230 C, 450 F, gas 8) for 20 minutes. Serve immediately.

Korma Rice

Serves 4–6

75 g/3 oz ghee
2 bay leaves
2 cinnamon sticks
4 green cardamoms
2 cloves
350 g/12 oz rice
2 pinches turmeric
salt to taste
900 ml/1½ pints plus 3 tablespoons water
2 tomatoes
3 cloves garlic
1-cm/½-in piece fresh root ginger, grated

450 g/1 lb mixed vegetables – for example, French beans, carrots, peas and sweet corn
2 onions, grated
½ teaspoon ground cumin
½ teaspoon ground coriander
1 teaspoon chilli powder
½ teaspoon sugar
1 tablespoon chopped cashew nuts
1 tablespoon poppy seeds
200 ml/7 fl oz milk
2 tablespoons single cream

1 Melt just less than half the ghee in a saucepan, then add the bay leaves, cinnamon, 2 cardamoms and cloves. Cook for ½ minute.

2 Stir in the rice, turmeric, salt to taste and 900 ml/1½ pints water. Bring to the boil, cover the pan and reduce the heat. Cook for 15–20 minutes or until the rice is tender.

3 When the rice is cooked, drain off the water (if necessary) and cool. Each grain of the cooked rice should be separate.

4 Place the tomatoes in a bowl, cover with boiling water. Allow to stand for 1 minute, then drain, peel and chop.

5 Grind the garlic with the ginger to make a paste.

6 Prepare and cook the mixed vegetables according to their type, cutting any large ones into bite-sized pieces.

7 Melt the remaining ghee and fry the grated onions in it until lightly browned. Add the garlic paste, cumin, coriander and chilli powder. Fry for 1 minute. Add the tomatoes and sugar, then fry for a further 3–4 minutes.

8 Stir in the vegetables, 3 tablespoons water and salt to taste. Cook for 2 minutes.

9 Grind the cashew nuts and poppy seeds together, then stir into the milk, add the cream and pour the mixture into the vegetables.

10 Cook for a few minutes, then layer this vegetable korma with the rice in an ovenproof dish. Begin and end with a layer of rice.

11 Bake, covered with cooking foil, in a hot oven (230 C, 450 F, gas 8) for 20 minutes. Turn out and serve immediately.

Baked Rice with Green Curry

Serves 4–6

275 g/10 oz long-grain rice
50 g/2 oz ghee
$\frac{1}{2}$ teaspoon black cumin seeds
2 cinnamon sticks
2 cloves
salt to taste
large bunch of fresh coriander
leaves, trimmed
7 green chillies
1 onion, chopped
4 cloves garlic
2.5-cm/1-in piece fresh root ginger,
grated

1 tablespoon chopped fresh mint
1 tablespoon poppy seeds
juice of $\frac{1}{2}$ lemon
2 green cardamoms
100 g/4 oz peas
150 g/5 oz paneer (page 122), cut into
small pieces
150 ml/$\frac{1}{4}$ pint natural yogurt
$\frac{1}{2}$ teaspoon sugar
GARNISH (optional)
boiled green peas
potato sticks or lightly crushed
crisps

1 Cook the rice according to the instructions on page 123 and allow to cool.

2 Melt half the ghee in a saucepan, add the black cumin seeds, cinnamon and cloves. Fry for $\frac{1}{2}$ minute. Add the rice and salt to taste. Set aside.

3 Grind the coriander leaves, chillies, onion, garlic, ginger, mint, poppy seeds and lemon juice to make a paste.

4 Melt the remaining ghee, add the paste and cardamoms, then fry for 2 minutes and remove from the heat. Add the peas, paneer, yogurt, sugar and salt to taste. Mix well.

5 Layer the two mixtures in a greased ovenproof dish. Make three layers of each, beginning and ending with the rice mixture. Cover with cooking foil and bake in a hot oven (230 C, 450 F, gas 8) for 20 minutes.

6 Turn the dish upside down on a big serving plate.

7 Surround the baked rice with freshly cooked peas. Sprinkle the potato sticks or crisps on the top and sides. Serve hot.

Baked Coconut Rice with Moglai Curry

Serves 4–6

1 fresh coconut
600 ml/1 pint hot water
3 onions, sliced
50 g/2 oz ghee
2 cinnamon sticks
2 cloves
275 g/10 oz long-grain rice
salt to taste
1 kg/2 lb mixed vegetables – for example cauliflower, courgettes, French beans, carrots and potatoes

3 tomatoes
1 teaspoon finely grated fresh root ginger
3 cloves garlic, crushed
$\frac{1}{2}$ teaspoon turmeric
2 teaspoons ground coriander
1$\frac{1}{2}$ teaspoons chilli powder
1 teaspoon garam masala (page 124)
200 ml/7 fl oz milk
3 tablespoons single cream

1 Pierce two of the eyes in the top of the coconut. Drain off the coconut water. Crack the nut open and grate the flesh. Place the grated coconut in a bowl with the hot water and allow to stand for a little while. Blend in a liquidiser and strain through a sieve to make coconut milk.

2 Slice one of the onions and grate the remaining two. Melt half the ghee in a saucepan and fry the sliced onion in it for 1 minute. Add the cinnamon and cloves and fry again for a little while.

3 Add the rice, coconut milk and salt to taste. Bring just to the boil, then cover and cook slowly until the rice is cooked – about 20 minutes. Add extra water during cooking if necessary.

4 Prepare and cook the vegetables according to their type. Drain and set aside.

5 Meanwhile, place the tomatoes in a bowl and cover with boiling water. Leave to stand for 1 minute, then peel and chop.

6 Melt the remaining ghee, add the grated onions and fry for a few minutes. Add the ginger and garlic, then fry for $\frac{1}{2}$ minute. Stir in the chopped tomatoes, turmeric, ground coriander, chilli powder, garam masala and salt to taste. Fry for at least 3–4 minutes. Add the vegetables, milk and cream and cook for a few minutes.

7 Layer the rice and curry in a greased ovenproof dish, beginning and ending with rice. Cover and bake in a hot oven (230 C, 450 F, gas 8) for 20 minutes.

8 Serve hot with fried papadums (page 77).

Masala Khichadi with Curry Sauce

Serves 6–8

350 g/12 oz masoor dal
350 g/12 oz long-grain rice
3 tablespoons grated fresh coconut
5 cloves garlic
2 teaspoons chopped fresh coriander
leaves
1 teaspoon cumin seeds
4 green cardamoms
2.5-cm/1-in piece fresh root ginger,
grated
6 mild red chillies
$\frac{1}{2}$ teaspoon turmeric
50 g/2 oz ghee
salt to taste
CURRY SAUCE
3 large tomatoes
1 teaspoon sugar
salt to taste

300 ml/$\frac{1}{2}$ pint water
2 large onions, chopped
1 tablespoon chopped cashew nuts
1 tablespoon chopped almonds
(optional)
1 tablespoon coriander seeds
1 tablespoon poppy seeds
2 teaspoons aniseeds
2 tablespoons grated fresh coconut
2.5-cm/1-in piece fresh root ginger
2 green chillies
4 red chillies
3 green cardamoms
3 cloves
3 cinnamon sticks
7 curry leaves
50 g/2 oz ghee
a few saffron strands

1 Soak the masoor dal overnight in enough cold water to cover.

2 Next day, cook the dal according to the instructions on page 123. When cooked, drain and set aside. Meanwhile, cook the rice according to the instructions on page 123. Allow to cool.

3 Grind the coconut with the garlic, chopped coriander, cumin seeds, cardamoms, ginger, chillies and turmeric to make a paste.

4 Melt the ghee in a saucepan, add the paste and cook for 3–4 minutes. To make up the khichadi, add the rice, dal and salt to taste and mix well.

5 To make the curry sauce, cut the tomatoes into quarters and place them in a saucepan with the sugar, salt to taste and water. Bring to the boil and cook until soft and pulpy. Press through a sieve.

6 Grind all the remaining ingredients except for the ghee and saffron to make a paste.

7 Melt the ghee in a saucepan, add the paste and fry for at least 4 minutes. Add the tomato liquid and heat through.

8 Warm the saffron in a small basin over hot water. Add a little milk and rub the saffron until it dissolves. Add to the curry sauce. Serve the hot sauce in a dish to accompany the khichadi.

Note: Both the khichadi and the curry sauce can be served as separate dishes.

Side Dishes and Salads

No Indian meal would be complete without a selection of accompaniments, so here are a few recipes for salads and raitas, a chutney and papadums. Cool Cucumber Salad goes well with hot and spicy vegetable curries. With dry spiced dishes try a moist Fruit and Vegetable Raita or serve Coconut Curry Sauce. Crisp papadums are the simplest of accompaniments to prepare and they are delicious with all Indian food. Similarly, a bowl of Spicy Yogurt goes very well with most spiced dishes.

When you prepare the recipes in this chapter, look upon them as the final touches to complement the meal. For example, you can serve raitas and salads in small bowls or on attractive platters and where appropriate sprinkle a little chopped fresh coriander or a hint of chilli powder over them.

If you have the time, allow yogurt dishes and cool salads to chill lightly before they are served. However, if the vegetable is likely to become watery on standing, as in the case of cucumber, or if any ingredients may discolour, bananas for example, then it's best not to make the dish too far in advance.

Cucumber Salad

(Illustrated on pages 104/105)

Serves 4

2 tablespoons single cream
150 ml/$\frac{1}{4}$ pint natural yogurt
1 teaspoon mustard powder

2 green chillies, chopped
salt and sugar to taste
1 large cucumber, finely chopped

1 Mix the cream, yogurt, mustard, chillies, salt and sugar to taste.
2 Stir in the cucumber and chill for 2 hours before serving.

Banana Nut Salad

(Illustrated on page 85)

Serves 6

150 ml/$\frac{1}{4}$ pint single cream
3 tablespoons natural yogurt
1 teaspoon mustard powder
salt and sugar to taste
50 g/2 oz paneer (page 122),
crumbled

1 tablespoon chopped roasted
peanuts
6 small bananas
juice of $\frac{1}{2}$ lemon
1 small lettuce, trimmed and washed
2 carrots, grated

1 Mix the cream with the yogurt, mustard, salt and sugar to taste. Stir in the paneer and nuts. Chill for 10 minutes.
2 Slit the bananas lengthwise and sprinkle the lemon juice over them. Arrange the lettuce leaves on a serving dish, lay the bananas on top and pour over the yogurt mixture.
3 Sprinkle the grated carrots on top and serve as an accompaniment with vegetable curries.

Coconut Curry Sauce

(Illustrated on back cover and pages 20/21)

Serves 6

1 fresh coconut
600 ml/1 pint hot water
25 g/1 oz ghee
1 teaspoon cumin seeds
6 green chillies
a few curry leaves
1 onion, chopped

1 tablespoon chopped fresh
coriander leaves
1-cm/$\frac{1}{2}$-in piece fresh root ginger,
grated
$\frac{1}{2}$ teaspoon sugar
salt to taste

1 Pierce two of the eyes in the top of the coconut and drain off the coconut water. Break the nut in half with a hammer, remove and grate the flesh.

2 Reserve 2 tablespoons of the grated coconut. Add the hot water to the remaining coconut and allow to stand for a little while. Blend in a liquidiser and strain through a sieve to obtain coconut milk.

3 Melt the ghee in a saucepan, add the cumin seeds and fry for $\frac{1}{2}$ minute. Slit one of the chillies open and add it to the cumin with the curry leaves. Continue to fry for a few minutes.

4 Grind the reserved coconut, onion, remaining chillies, chopped coriander and ginger to a paste, then add the paste to the pan and continue to fry for a further 1 minute.

5 Stir in the coconut milk, sugar and salt. Bring to the boil, simmer for 10 minutes and serve hot with the Vegetable Ring (page 31).

Zesty Dip

(Illustrated on pages 92/93)

Serves 4

150 ml/$\frac{1}{4}$ pint thick natural yogurt
salt to taste
4 large radishes, grated

1 cucumber, grated
3 tablespoons single cream
2 green chillies, chopped

1 Line a basin with a piece of muslin. Pour in the yogurt and tie the muslin around it. Hang the yogurt over a basin for 1 hour.

2 Sprinkle salt over the grated radish and cucumber in a colander and leave to stand over a bowl for 30 minutes. Squeeze out the water and dry the vegetables on absorbent kitchen paper.

3 Mix the yogurt, cream, chillies, radish, cucumber and salt to taste, then chill thoroughly before serving.

4 Serve as a dip with warm crackers or papadums (page 77). Alternatively serve as a side dish with curries.

Fruit and Vegetable Raita

(Illustrated on pages 56/57)

Serves 6

300 ml/½ pint thick natural yogurt
2 tablespoons double cream
50 g/2 oz grapes
100 g/4 oz chopped cabbage
1 banana, sliced

2 dessert apples, cored and chopped
1 cucumber, chopped
2 green chillies, chopped
2 teaspoons cumin seeds
2 teaspoons sugar

1 Lightly whisk the yogurt with the cream. Halve the grapes and remove their seeds, then mix them with the remaining ingredients.
2 Stir these mixed ingredients into the whisked yogurt and pour into a bowl. Chill lightly before serving.

Palak Raita

Serves 6

450 g/1 lb fresh spinach leaves or 1
(227-g/8-oz) packet frozen spinach
2 green chillies, chopped
2 pinches pepper

2 pinches sugar
1 teaspoon salt
450 ml/¾ pint natural yogurt
a little chilli powder

1 Cook the fresh spinach in boiling water, then drain thoroughly and finely chop it. Cook the frozen spinach, if used, according to the instructions on the packet and drain thoroughly.
2 Stir the spinach, chillies, pepper, sugar and salt into the yogurt and chill thoroughly before serving sprinkled with a little chilli powder.

Spicy Yogurt

(*Illustrated on page 100*)

Serves 6

3 tablespoons chopped fresh mint
leaves
1 tablespoon water
450 ml/$\frac{3}{4}$ pint natural yogurt
1 tablespoon finely chopped fresh
coriander leaves

1 teaspoon sugar
1 teaspoon salt
1 teaspoon cumin seeds
a little chilli powder

1 Grind or purée the mint with the water, then beat into the yogurt and add the coriander, sugar and salt.

2 Lightly roast the cumin seeds in a heavy-based frying pan, then grind them to a powder and add to the yogurt mixture. Stir well to make sure all the ingredients are combined.

3 Chill the mixture thoroughly. If you like, sprinkle a little chilli powder over before the spicy yogurt is served.

Green Chutney

1 bunch fresh coriander leaves
4 green chillies
4 tablespoons grated fresh coconut

1 teaspoon salt
3 teaspoons sugar
1$\frac{1}{2}$ teaspoons lemon juice

1 Trim most of the stalks off the coriander and place the leaves in a liquidiser.

2 Add the remaining ingredients and blend them together to form a paste, adding a little water if necessary. Use either as an accompaniment or as required in the recipes.

Note: Fresh chutney does not store very well but it can be kept in a covered container in the refrigerator for a few days.

Papadums

(*Illustrated on pages 52/53 and 85*)

There are numerous varieties of papadums available, sold in packets ready for cooking. You can either roast papadums directly over a gas flame or under a hot grill. Alternatively they can be deep or shallow fried in oil until crisp.

If you like, before serving the cooked papadums sprinkle a little chilli powder on top. Alternatively, sprinkle fresh coriander and grated coconut over them.

Gado Gado

(Illustrated on page 29)

Serves 8–10

100 g/4 oz long-grain rice
350 ml/12 fl oz water
salt to taste
10 French beans, diagonally sliced
3 carrots, coarsely grated
100 g/4 oz bean sprouts
100 g/4 oz cabbage, shredded
1 cucumber, cut into matchstick
strips
2 tomatoes, thinly sliced
2 teaspoons caster sugar
1½ teaspoons salt
a little pepper

DRESSING
2 tablespoons oil
1 onion, chopped
100 g/4 oz salted peanuts
1 tablespoon chopped tamarind
1 tablespoon molasses
1–1½ teaspoons chilli powder
300 ml/½ pint water
salt to taste
3 tablespoons single cream
GARNISH
2 onions, sliced and fried
a few cooked papadums (page 77),
crushed
a little chilli powder or fried
chopped chillies

1 Place the rice in a saucepan with the water and a generous pinch of salt. Bring to the boil, cover the pan and reduce the heat. Cook gently for about 15–20 minutes or until all the water has been absorbed. Allow to cool.

2 Lightly cook the French beans in boiling salted water. Drain the beans and place them in a large bowl.

3 Mix the carrots, bean sprouts, cabbage, cucumber and tomatoes with the beans. Season with the sugar, salt and pepper, mix well and chill.

4 To make the dressing, heat the oil in a saucepan, add the chopped onion and cook until soft. Allow to cool.

5 Grind the peanuts, tamarind, molasses, chilli powder and onion together to make a paste. Gradually blend in the water, salt and cream.

6 Arrange the vegetable mixture on a large serving dish and top with the rice.

7 Pour the dressing over the rice. Top with the fried onions, papadums and a little chilli powder. Serve immediately.

Breads

Breads play an important part in the Indian menu, for they are used as an implement to scoop up the food from the plate and mop up the rich sauces.

Several types of bread are included in this chapter. In preparation, the dough can be kneaded and rolled several times, with or without a raising agent, then shaped into rounds, ovals or triangular pancakes. Some breads are deep-fried in ghee, others are dry fried on a tava or griddle and certain varieties are baked. Whatever the cooking method the end result should be light and browned, often puffed or crisp, and the bread should always be served freshly cooked.

Spicy vegetable stuffings are added in some recipes to give satisfying moist breads which are absolutely delicious. And there is also a recipe for a sweet bread – Nariyal ni Mithi Rotli. This is served with savoury dishes and the result is quite mouth watering.

Parathas

Makes 10–12

450 g/1 lb wholemeal flour
½ teaspoon salt
50 g/2 oz ghee

350 ml/12 fl oz water
about 50 g/2 oz ghee, melted to
brush over the dough

1 Sift the flour into a bowl with the salt. Rub in the ghee, then gradually mix in the water to make a soft dough.

2 Divide the dough into 10–12 equal portions and shape each into a ball. Roll each ball of dough into a circle measuring about 13–15 cm/5–6 in. in diameter.

3 Brush each round with melted ghee and fold in half. Brush with more melted ghee and fold into quarters. Roll out the folded dough once more, into rounds similar in size to the original circles.

4 Cook one round at a time on a hot griddle or heavy-based frying pan, turning once. After 1 minute brush a little extra ghee around the edges – they should puff up.

5 Turn the paratha and fry the other side. The bread is ready when browned on both sides.

Chapatis

(*Illustrated on page 17*)

Makes 8–10

225 g/8 oz wholemeal flour   2 teaspoons oil or ghee   about 150 ml/¼ pint water

1 Sift the flour into a bowl, add the oil or ghee and gradually mix in the water to make a soft dough. Knead the dough for a few minutes, then set it aside in a covered bowl for 30 minutes.

2 Break off small pieces of the dough and roll them out on a floured surface to make thin circles.

3 Cook the chapatis on a hot griddle or heavy-based frying pan for a few seconds on one side. Turn and cook the other side for a few seconds.

4 Holding the chapati with tongs, finish cooking it directly over a gas flame until it puffs up like a ball. Alternatively place the bread under a hot grill.

5 Flatten, spread with a little ghee and serve hot.

Paneer Mutter Korma (page 44) and Saffron Pullao (page 67)

Potato Roti

(Illustrated on page 104/105)

Makes 4

3 large potatoes, boiled and mashed
2 tablespoons chopped fresh
coriander leaves
3 green chillies, chopped

25 g/1 oz butter, melted
1 teaspoon salt
about 100 g/4 oz plain flour
ghee for frying

1 Mix all the ingredients thoroughly, adding enough flour to make a soft dough. Water is not required for this purpose.

2 Divide the dough into four equal portions, then roll each on a floured surface to give a round measuring about 15 cm/6 in. in diameter.

3 Heat a griddle or heavy-based frying pan. Cook the roti dry on the hot surface, or first grease the pan with a little ghee.

4 When the underside is browned, turn the roti over and cook on the second side. Serve immediately with curry or dal.

5 Alternatively, the roti can be deep fried in hot ghee.

Sabji Parathas

Makes 8

225 g/8 oz plain flour
$\frac{1}{2}$ teaspoon salt
2 teaspoons melted butter
150 ml/$\frac{1}{4}$ pint milk
STUFFING
2 tablespoons ghee
1 onion, finely chopped
175 g/6 oz cooked vegetables – for
example, French beans, carrots and
peas

1 small potato, boiled and finely
chopped
salt to taste
2 green chillies, chopped
$\frac{1}{2}$ teaspoon chilli powder
2 pinches garam masala (page 124)
2 tablespoons chopped fresh
coriander leaves
ghee for cooking

1 Sift the flour and salt into a bowl. Mix the butter and milk to make a soft dough, adding a little extra milk if necessary. Knead the dough thoroughly on a lightly floured surface.

2 To make the stuffing, melt the ghee in a frying pan. Add the onion and cook until soft.

3 Finely chop the cooked vegetables and add to the pan with the potato, salt, chillies, chilli powder, garam masala and chopped coriander. Cook for 1 minute, then cool the mixture.

4 Divide the dough into eight equal portions and roll out very thinly into 15-cm/6-in circles.

5 Put 2 tablespoons of stuffing in the centre of each paratha. Fold in half to make a semi-circle, pressing the edges together to keep the filling in.

6 Heat a griddle or heavy-based frying pan and cook the parathas on one side only. Fold into quarters, turning the cooked side inside.

7 Spread more ghee on top, turn over and cook, turning once, until browned on both sides. Serve immediately.

Khamiri Pea Puris

(Illustrated on pages 24/25)

Makes 8

175 g/6 oz plain flour	1 teaspoon cumin seeds
175 g/6 oz wholemeal flour	2 tablespoons chopped fresh
15 g/½ oz fresh yeast or 1 teaspoon	coriander leaves
dried yeast	6–7 green chillies, chopped
1 teaspoon sugar	4 teaspoons mango powder
250 ml/8 fl oz lukewarm water	175 g/6 oz peas, cooked and mashed
2 tablespoons melted ghee	ghee for cooking
1 teaspoon salt	

1 Mix the flours in a bowl and make a well in the centre.

2 Cream the fresh yeast with the sugar. Pour in half the water and allow to stand for about 5 minutes or until frothy. If using dried yeast, sprinkle it over the water and sugar in a jug and allow to stand for 5–10 minutes until dissolved and frothy. Pour into the well in the flour.

3 Add half the ghee, salt and remaining water. Gradually stir the flour into the yeast liquid to make a soft dough.

4 Knead the dough thoroughly until smooth and elastic.

5 Place the dough in a floured bowl and cover with a damp cloth or cling film. Leave to stand in a warm place for 30 minutes.

6 Meanwhile, prepare the stuffing. Heat the remaining ghee in a frying pan and fry the cumin seeds in it for 1 minute. Add all the remaining ingredients, season to taste and mix well. Set aside to cool.

7 Divide the dough into eight equal portions. Roll out each to give a 10-cm/4-in circle. Place a little of the filling in the middle of the rolled out dough and fold the edges up to enclose the pea mixture completely.

8 Flatten the stuffed dough and roll out to give a 10-cm/4-in round. Repeat with the remaining dough and stuffing. Leave the prepared puris to stand on a floured board for 10–15 minutes.

9 Melt enough ghee to give a 2.5-cm/1-in depth of fat in a deep frying pan or saucepan.

10 Fry the puris one at a time until golden brown, turning once to brown both sides. Drain on absorbent kitchen paper and serve immediately.

Vegetable-stuffed Puris

Makes 10

2 slices bread
350 g/12 oz plain flour
$\frac{1}{2}$ teaspoon salt
1 tablespoon melted ghee
350 ml/12 fl oz water
ghee for deep frying
6–7 potatoes, boiled and mashed
75 g/3 oz peas, cooked and mashed
3 green chillies, chopped
2 teaspoons garam masala (page 124)
1 teaspoon lemon juice
salt to taste
about 50 g/2 oz dry breadcrumbs
oil for deep frying

MASALA WATER
2 teaspoons mango powder
1 teaspoon chilli powder
$\frac{1}{2}$ teaspoon garam masala (page 124)
$\frac{1}{4}$ teaspoon salt
150 ml/$\frac{1}{4}$ pint water
ONION MASALA
1 teaspoon chilli powder
1 teaspoon mango powder
$\frac{1}{2}$ teaspoon salt
1 large onion, finely chopped
ghee for cooking
Chillies in vinegar (page 16) to serve

1 Cut the crusts off the bread and soak the slices in water for a few minutes. Squeeze out the water and crumble the bread into a bowl.

2 Sift 250 g/9 oz of the flour and the $\frac{1}{2}$ teaspoon salt over the bread. Add the ghee and 150 ml/$\frac{1}{4}$ pint water, then mix and knead to make a dough.

3 Divide the dough into ten equal portions and roll into thick puris measuring about 15 cm/6 in. in diameter.

4 Heat the ghee for deep frying to 180 C/350 F, then fry the puris very lightly until puffed but not browned. Drain and set aside.

5 Mix the potatoes, peas, chillies, garam masala, lemon juice and salt to taste. Shape into long rolls about the size of frankfurters or sausages.

6 Make a batter by mixing the remaining flour and water with salt to taste. Dip the potato rolls in batter, then roll in the breadcrumbs.

7 Heat the oil for deep frying to 180 C/350 F, add the potato rolls and cook until golden brown. Drain on absorbent kitchen paper and keep hot.

8 To make the masala water, mix the mango and chilli powders, garam masala, salt and water.

9 Mix all the ingredients for the onion masala and set aside.

10 Heat a small, heavy-based frying pan and grease it lightly with ghee. Cook the puris again for a few minutes on each side until puffed and golden brown.

11 Brush a little masala water over each puri, sprinkle with a little of the onion masala and a few chillies in vinegar. Put a potato roll in the centre, fold the puris over and serve immediately.

Rajma Curry (page 51), Banana Nut Salad (page 74) and Papadums
(page 77)

Parathas Stuffed with Vegetables and Cheese

Makes 5–6

3 carrots
1 small cauliflower
2 potatoes
5 green chillies, chopped
4 tablespoons chopped fresh
coriander leaves
2.5-cm/1-in piece fresh root ginger,
grated
50 g/2 oz ghee

1 teaspoon cumin seeds
100 g/4 oz peas
350 ml/12 fl oz water
4 tablespoons grated Cheddar cheese
salt to taste
175 g/6 oz plain flour
175 g/6 oz wholemeal flour
$\frac{3}{4}$ teaspoon salt
ghee for cooking

1 Finely chop the carrots, cauliflower and potatoes.

2 Grind 3 chillies, 2 tablespoons of the chopped coriander and the grated ginger to make a paste.

3 Melt half the ghee in a saucepan, add the cumin seeds and fry for about 1 minute. Add the chopped vegetables, peas, paste and 6 tablespoons of the water. Bring to the boil, then cook gently until the vegetables become soft.

4 Roughly mash the vegetables, add the cheese, reserved chopped chillies, chopped coriander and salt. Mix well.

5 Mix the flours with the $\frac{3}{4}$ teaspoon salt and rub in the remaining ghee. Add enough of the remaining water to make a soft dough. Knead well, then divide into 10–12 portions.

6 Roll out the pieces of dough to give 15-cm/6-in circles. Place one dough circle on a heated, greased griddle or heavy-based frying pan, spread a little filling on top and cover with a second circle of dough, pressing the edges together well.

7 Spread a little ghee on top, turn the paratha over and spread more ghee on top. Cook until browned on the underside, then turn and cook until browned on the second side. Serve immediately.

Khamiri Parathas

Makes 5

175 g/6 oz plain flour
175 g/6 oz wholemeal flour
1 teaspoon baking powder
150 ml/¼ pint natural yogurt
1 teaspoon sugar
1 teaspoon salt
1 tablespoon melted ghee
150 ml/¼ pint water

STUFFING
salt
100 g/4 oz cabbage, finely shredded
100 g/4 oz cauliflower, grated
1 tablespoon chopped fresh
coriander leaves
3–4 green chillies, chopped
½ teaspoon finely chopped fresh root
ginger
ghee for cooking

1 Mix the flours in a bowl and make a well in the centre. Add the baking powder. Pour in the yogurt and leave to stand for 1 minute. Add the sugar, salt, ghee and water. Mix the ingredients to make a soft dough.

2 Knead the dough until smooth and set aside in a covered bowl for 3–4 hours.

3 Meanwhile, prepare the stuffing. Sprinkle salt over the shredded cabbage and grated cauliflower, then leave to stand for a few minutes. Squeeze out all the water and place the vegetables in a bowl. Add the chopped coriander, chillies, ginger and salt to taste. Mix well.

4 Divide the dough into ten equal portions and roll out each to give a 10-cm/4-in circle. Spread a little filling on one circle of dough, cover with a second circle and press together well. Roll out into a paratha measuring about 20 cm/8 in. in diameter. Repeat with the rest of the dough and stuffing.

5 Heat a griddle or heavy-based frying pan. Grease the pan with a little ghee. Cook the parathas, one at a time, until browned on the underside.

6 Spread a little ghee on the top of the paratha, then turn it over and cook until browned on the second side. Serve immediately.

Overleaf *From the left: Paneer Palak Parathas (page 90), Yogurt Kofta Curry (page 47) and Stuffed Potato and Paneer Pears (page 111) with natural yogurt, chopped tomatoes and grated carrot*

Paneer Palak Parathas

(Illustrated on pages 88/89)

Makes 6

1 (227-g/8-oz) packet frozen chopped
spinach, thawed
4 tablespoons water
$\frac{1}{2}$ teaspoon lemon juice
175 g/6 oz plain flour
175 g/6 oz wholemeal flour
25 g/1 oz ghee
1 teaspoon salt
STUFFING
100 g/4 oz cauliflower, grated

50 g/2 oz paneer (page 122),
crumbled
1 tablespoon chopped fresh
coriander leaves
3 green chillies, chopped
$\frac{1}{2}$ teaspoon finely chopped fresh root
ginger
salt to taste
ghee for cooking
natural yogurt to serve (optional)

1 Blend the spinach with 2 tablespoons of the water and lemon juice in a liquidiser.

2 Mix both the flours in a bowl and rub in the ghee. Add the salt.

3 Stir in the blended spinach and enough of the remaining water to make a soft dough.

4 Mix all the ingredients for the stuffing.

5 Divide the dough into six. Roll out each portion of the dough into a circle measuring about 15 cm/6 in. in diameter.

6 Put about 2–3 tablespoons of the stuffing in the centre and fold the edges up over the filling, pressing them together to seal in the mixture.

7 Roll out again to make a thick, 15-cm/6 in circle. Repeat with the rest of the dough and filling.

8 Heat a griddle or heavy-based frying pan and grease it generously with ghee. Cook the parathas on one side, spread ghee on top, then turn over and cook on the second side. Serve immediately with yogurt.

Koki

Makes 6–8

225 g/8 oz wholemeal flour
$\frac{3}{4}$ teaspoon salt
2 onions, chopped
2 tablespoons chopped fresh
coriander leaves
2–3 green chillies, chopped

1 teaspoon cumin seeds
1 teaspoon grated fresh root ginger
2 tablespoons melted ghee
about 150 ml/$\frac{1}{4}$ pint water
ghee for cooking

1 Sift the flour and salt into a bowl. Add all the remaining ingredients, mixing in the water to make a stiff dough.

2 Knead the dough lightly, then divide it into six or eight equal portions. Roll out each portion into a circle measuring about 15 cm/6 in. in diameter. Using a sharp knife make a few light, horizontal slits on one side of each koki.

3 Grease a griddle or heavy-based frying pan with ghee and cook the breads, turning once, until browned on both sides. Serve hot.

Indian Teacakes

(Illustrated on page 100)

Makes 6

250 g/9 oz plain flour
$\frac{3}{4}$ teaspoon salt
15 g/$\frac{1}{2}$ oz fresh yeast
$\frac{3}{4}$ teaspoon sugar
200 ml/7 fl oz warm water
2 teaspoons melted ghee
25 g/1 oz ghee
1 onion, chopped
225 g/8 oz cooked mixed vegetables, chopped

1 potato, boiled and chopped
2–3 green chillies, chopped
1 teaspoon chilli powder
$\frac{1}{2}$ teaspoon garam masala (page 124)
2 tablespoons chopped fresh coriander leaves
melted ghee or butter to serve

1 Sift the flour and salt into a bowl and make a well in the centre. Cream the yeast and sugar with a little of the warm water, then add the remaining water. Leave to stand for about 10 minutes or until the yeast liquid is frothy.

2 Pour the liquid into the bowl then mix in the flour and add the melted ghee to make a soft dough. Knead the dough for 5 minutes.

3 Place the dough in a greased bowl and cover with a damp cloth. Allow to rise for 25 minutes or until doubled in size.

4 Meanwhile, melt the 25 g/1 oz ghee in a saucepan and fry the onion in it for 1 minute.

5 Add the vegetables, chillies, chilli powder, garam masala and chopped coriander. Cook for 1 minute, then remove from the heat and allow to cool.

6 Quickly knead the risen dough and divide into six portions. Roll each portion into a 10-cm/4-in round. Divide the filling between the bread circles and fold the edges up around it.

7 Seal the edges of the dough, then flatten the breads into 15-cm/6-in rounds.

8 Leave to rise in a warm place for 20–25 minutes, then bake in a hot oven (230 C, 450 F, gas 8) for 10 minutes and serve hot, brushed with ghee or butter.

Overleaf *From the left: Papadums (page 77), Three-in-one Rice (page 62), Zesty Dip (page 75) and Bread Koftas in Pumpkin Curry (page 43)*

Methi Roti

Makes 6–8

225 g/8 oz wholemeal flour
1 teaspoon salt
1 bunch fresh fenugreek leaves,
finely chopped
1 teaspoon cumin seeds

2 tablespoons chopped fresh
coriander leaves
2–3 green chillies, chopped
$\frac{1}{2}$ teaspoon chilli powder
about 150 ml/$\frac{1}{4}$ pint natural yogurt
ghee or oil for cooking

1 Sift the flour and salt into a bowl. Add the remaining ingredients and, if required, a little additional yogurt or water to make a dough.

2 Knead the dough lightly, then divide it into six or eight portions. Roll out each portion into a circle measuring about 15 cm/6 in. in diameter.

3 Grease a heavy-based frying pan or griddle with ghee or oil and cook the roti, turning once, until browned on both sides. Serve hot.

Nariyal ni Mithi Rotli

Makes about 10

2 teaspoons ghee
100 g/4 oz fresh coconut, grated
75 g/3 oz caster sugar
$\frac{1}{2}$ teaspoon ground cardamom
$\frac{1}{2}$ teaspoon grated nutmeg

DOUGH
350 g/12 oz wholemeal flour
pinch of salt
1 tablespoon melted ghee
about 200–250 ml/7–8 fl oz water
ghee for cooking

1 Melt the ghee in a small frying pan. Add the coconut and cook gently, stirring continuously until it is lightly coloured and totally dry. This takes 15–20 minutes. Set aside to cool.

2 Stir the sugar, ground cardamom and nutmeg into the coconut. Taste and add extra sugar and nutmeg as desired.

3 Sift the flour and salt for the dough into a bowl. Make a well in the centre, then add the ghee and enough water to make a fairly soft dough. Allow to stand, covered, for 30 minutes.

4 Divide the dough into about 20 portions, then roll out each into small circles measuring about 10 cm/4 in. in diameter. Keep the un-rolled dough covered with cling-film or a damp cloth.

5 Spread about 1 tablespoon of the filling on each of half the circles of dough and dampen the edges. Press the remaining circles of dough on top, sealing the edges to enclose the filling completely.

6 Grease a griddle or heavy-based frying pan and cook the breads, turning once until browned on both sides. Serve with Green Peas Ambti (page 36).

Snacks

Here is a selection of imaginative recipes using vegetables, dals and rice. As well as being ideal for light meals, many of these dishes can be served as accompaniments for the main meal.

Neat patties, savoury cakes and balls cooked in a very light batter or breadcrumbs form the majority of recipes in this chapter. They are easily eaten with the fingers, deliciously spiced and offer an excellent contrast in food textures.

If you would like to serve a separate first course to open the meal, then many of the recipes in this chapter would make tasty starters – Vegetable Rolls, for example, are interesting pancakes filled with a chutney, salad and a deep-fried vegetable mixture.

Whenever you want a snack to eat between meals, or if you feel in doubt as to how best to complete your menu, try one or two of these well-flavoured, interesting and quite satisfying savouries.

Semolina Pancakes

(Illustrated on page 64)

Makes about 18

275 g/10 oz semolina
200 ml/7 fl oz natural yogurt
200 ml/7 fl oz water
100 g/4 oz frozen sweet corn, cooked
1 tablespoon chopped fresh
coriander leaves

4–5 green chillies, chopped
$\frac{1}{2}$ teaspoon bicarbonate of soda
2 teaspoons ghee or oil
2 pinches asafoetida
salt to taste
ghee or oil for cooking

1 Mix the semolina, yogurt and water together in a bowl and allow to stand for at least 5–6 hours.

2 Add all the remaining ingredients and mix together thoroughly to form a batter.

3 Melt the ghee or heat the oil in a non-stick frying pan. Drop spoonfuls of the batter into the pan and cook until browned on one side, turn over and cook the second side. Serve hot.

Note: When the pancakes are cooked on one side, they can be sprinkled with finely chopped carrots and chopped fresh coriander leaves. Turn over and cook the second side.

Bread Snack

Serves 4

2 tablespoons oil
2 teaspoons mustard seeds
10–12 slices bread, made into
crumbs
2 onions, chopped
2 curry leaves
2 tomatoes, chopped
4–5 green chillies, chopped

1 teaspoon finely chopped fresh root
ginger
1 tablespoon concentrated tomato
purée
juice of 1 lemon
2 tablespoons chopped fresh
coriander leaves
salt to taste

1 Heat the oil in a frying pan and fry the mustard seeds for $\frac{1}{2}$ minute. Add the breadcrumbs, onions and curry leaves, then continue to fry until the onions are lightly browned.

2 Add the tomatoes, chillies and ginger. Fry for 1 minute. Stir in the tomato purée, lemon juice, coriander and salt to taste. Cook stirring for 2–3 minutes.

3 Serve immediately, in small portions as a snack or accompaniment with vegetable curries.

Tomato Medley

Serves 2

4 tomatoes
1 large potato
25 g/1 oz butter
2 cloves garlic, crushed
1 onion, chopped
pinch of ajwain seeds

½ teaspoon chilli powder
2 teaspoons sugar
salt to taste
3 tablespoons grated Cheddar cheese
50 g/2 oz button mushrooms,
chopped

1 Place the tomatoes in a bowl and pour in enough boiling water to cover them. Allow to stand for 1 minute, then drain, peel and chop the tomatoes.

2 Cut the potato into small cubes.

3 Melt the butter and fry the garlic and onion in it for 1 minute. Stir in the tomatoes, potato, ajwain seeds, chilli powder, sugar and salt. Cook for a few minutes until the potato cubes are soft.

4 Stir in the grated cheese and chopped mushrooms and serve immediately.

Mee Goreng

Serves 4

225 g/8 oz egg noodles
5 large onions
5 cloves garlic
6 dried red chillies
1-cm/½-in piece fresh root ginger,
grated
6 tablespoons oil

4 tomatoes, chopped
100 g/4 oz bean sprouts
225 g/8 oz cabbage, shredded
3–4 tablespoons tomato ketchup
(optional)
salt to taste
½ cucumber, sliced

1 Cook the noodles in plenty of boiling salted water, drain and set aside.

2 Chop two of the onions and grind them to a paste with the garlic, chillies and ginger. Slice the remaining onions.

3 Heat the oil and fry the sliced onions until they are lightly browned. Add the paste and fry for a further 2–3 minutes. Add the tomatoes and cook for 1 minute.

4 Stir in the bean sprouts and cabbage, then continue to cook for 2 minutes. Add the noodles, tomato ketchup and salt. Mix well. Cook for a few minutes until heated through, then serve hot with the sliced cucumber.

Vegetarian Kababs

Serves 4

450 g/1 lb white pumpkin or
marrow, grated
2 onions, grated
2 medium potatoes, grated
salt
4 tablespoons gram flour
2 tablespoons chopped fresh
coriander leaves

5 green chillies, chopped
1 teaspoon black cumin seeds
oil for deep frying
MASALA
1 teaspoon chilli powder
1 teaspoon mango powder
$\frac{1}{2}$ teaspoon salt
2 onions, chopped

1 Place the grated pumpkin or marrow, onions and potatoes in a colander. Sprinkle 2 teaspoons of salt over them and leave to stand for 20 minutes. Squeeze all the water out of the vegetables and place them in a bowl.

2 Add salt to taste, the gram flour, coriander leaves, chillies and black cumin seeds. Shape the mixture into small balls about the size of walnuts. Meanwhile, heat the oil for deep frying to 180 C/350 F, then fry the balls a few at a time until golden.

3 Drain the kababs on absorbent kitchen paper and, while they are still hot, flatten them with a palette knife or spatula to form little cakes.

4 Mix all the ingredients for the masala.

5 To serve, deep fry the kababs to reheat them and sprinkle with the masala.

Vegetable Croquettes

Makes 24

100 g/4 oz plus 4 tablespoons plain
flour
salt to taste
300 ml/$\frac{1}{2}$ pint water
2 medium potatoes
2 carrots
225 g/8 oz French beans
450 g/1 lb cabbage
25 g/1 oz ghee

2 onions, finely chopped
$\frac{1}{2}$ teaspoon turmeric
2 pinches bicarbonate of soda
1 tablespoon chopped fresh
coriander leaves
4–5 green chillies, chopped
about 50 g/2 oz vermicelli, broken
into small pieces
ghee for deep frying

1 Make a batter by mixing the 100 g/4 oz flour and a pinch of salt with the water. Beat thoroughly until smooth and set aside.

2 Chop the potatoes, carrots, French beans and cabbage very finely.

3 Melt the ghee in a saucepan and fry the onions in it for a few minutes. Add the prepared vegetables, turmeric, bicarbonate of soda and salt to taste. Cover and cook gently until soft – about 30 minutes.

4 Sprinkle the 4 tablespoons flour over the vegetables and cook for 2 minutes. Remove the pan from the heat. Add the chopped coriander and chillies and mix well. Allow the mixture to cool, lightly flour your hands and shape the mixture into croquettes.

5 Lightly beat the batter. Dip the croquettes in the batter, then roll in the broken vermicelli.

6 Heat the ghee for deep frying to 180 C/350 F and cook the croquettes until golden browned. Drain on absorbent kitchen paper and serve immediately.

Sabzi Wadas

Makes 15

2 onions, chopped
3–4 green chillies
2.5-cm/1-in piece of fresh root ginger, grated
25 g/1 oz ghee
1 tomato, chopped
1 teaspoon chilli powder (optional)
2 tablespoons chopped fresh coriander leaves
a few mint leaves, chopped
450 g/1 lb mixed vegetables – for example French beans, aubergines and carrots – cooked and finely chopped

3 large potatoes, boiled and coarsely mashed
salt to taste
50 g/2 oz plain flour
150 ml/$\frac{1}{4}$ pint water
about 50 g/2 oz dry breadcrumbs
oil for deep frying
chilli sauce to serve (optional)

1 Grind half the chopped onion with the chillies and ginger to make a paste.

2 Melt the ghee in a saucepan, add the remaining onion and fry for a few minutes. Add the paste and continue to cook for 2 minutes. Add the tomato, chilli powder (if used), chopped coriander and mint. Cook for 2 minutes.

3 Stir in the vegetables, mashed potatoes and salt to taste. Mix thoroughly, then allow to cool.

4 Mix the flour and water to make a batter and beat well until smooth.

5 Shape spoonfuls of the vegetable mixture into balls about the size of a small egg. Dip the vegetable balls first in the batter, then roll them lightly in the breadcrumbs.

6 Heat the oil for deep frying to 180 C/350 F and fry the balls until golden. Serve hot with chilli sauce.

Vegetable Rolls

(Illustrated on pages 24/25)

Makes 6

4–5 medium potatoes, boiled and
coarsely mashed
2 tablespoons chopped fresh
coriander leaves
3–4 green chillies, chopped
2 teaspoons lemon juice
1 teaspoon garam masala (page 124)
salt to taste
50 g/2 oz gram flour
175 g/6 oz plain flour
300 ml/$\frac{1}{2}$ pint water
chilli powder to taste
1 teaspoon baking powder
300 ml/$\frac{1}{2}$ pint milk

ghee for frying
oil for deep frying
CHUTNEY
large bunch of fresh coriander
leaves, trimmed
3–4 green chillies, chopped
$\frac{3}{4}$ teaspoon sugar
$\frac{1}{2}$ teaspoon salt
3 tablespoons grated fresh coconut
juice of $\frac{1}{2}$ lemon
SALAD
1 small lettuce, shredded
1 small onion, chopped
2 carrots, grated

1 Mix the potatoes, chopped coriander, chillies, lemon juice, garam masala, and salt to taste. Shape into rolls about 2.5 cm/1 in. in diameter and 7.5–10 cm/3–4 in. in length.

2 Mix the gram flour with 50 g/2 oz of the plain flour and beat in the water to make a batter. Add salt and chilli powder to taste.

3 Mix the remaining plain flour with the baking powder and a pinch of salt. Beat in the milk to make a smooth batter.

4 Melt a little ghee in a non-stick frying pan. Pour in a little of the milk batter to make fairly thick pancakes measuring about 15 cm/6 in. in diameter. Cook until browned underneath, then turn over and cook the second side. Continue until all the batter is used. Layer the pancakes with kitchen paper to prevent them sticking. Keep hot.

5 To make the chutney grind the coriander with the chillies, sugar, salt, coconut and lemon juice to form a paste.

6 Heat the oil for deep frying to 180 C/350F. Dip the potato rolls in the prepared water batter and deep fry until golden.

7 Mix the salad ingredients.

8 Spread a little chutney over each pancake. Top with a little of the salad and a potato roll. Fold over and serve.

Masala Dal (page 50), Indian Teacakes (page 91) and Spicy Yogurt (page 77)

Green Peas Renedy

(Illustrated on back cover and pages 56/57)

Makes 6

450 g/1 lb peas
10 green chillies, chopped
175 g/6 oz paneer (page 122)
salt to taste
6 teaspoons oil
5 potatoes, boiled and mashed
$\frac{1}{4}$ teaspoon turmeric

2 pinches bicarbonate of soda
juice of 2 lemons
$\frac{1}{2}$ teaspoon sugar
75 g/3 oz plain flour
200 ml/7 fl oz water
75 g/3 oz dry breadcrumbs
oil for deep frying

1 Mash the peas with the chillies. Grate the paneer, then mash it with salt to taste. Shape the paneer into six small balls about the size of walnuts.

2 Heat half the oil in a saucepan, add the mashed potatoes, turmeric and salt to taste. Mix well and cool.

3 Heat the remaining oil in another saucepan. Add the peas, bicarbonate of soda, lemon juice, sugar and salt to taste. Cook for a few minutes. Cool the mixture.

4 Shape spoonfuls of the potato mixture into thin round cakes measuring about 7.5–10 cm/3–4 in. in diameter. Put a paneer ball in each and fold the potato around it to enclose the paneer completely. Knead lightly until smooth. Press a layer of the pea mixture around the potatoes.

5 Mix the flour and water to a smooth batter, beating thoroughly until smooth. Dip the balls in the batter, then roll in the breadcrumbs.

6 Heat the oil for deep frying to 180 C/350 F, add the balls and cook until golden brown. Drain on absorbent kitchen paper, cut in half and serve immediately.

Corn Pancakes

Makes 15–20

12 cobs of corn
4 tablespoons plain flour
$\frac{1}{4}$ teaspoon baking powder
4 tablespoons single cream
4 tablespoons milk
1 teaspoon melted butter
1 tablespoon chopped fresh
coriander leaves

3–4 green chillies, chopped
salt to taste
ghee for cooking
TO SERVE
a little butter
Green Chutney (page 77)

1 Strip off and reserve the husks from the corn. Discard the silky threads. Place the cobs in boiling salted water and simmer for 10–15 minutes, or until the corn is tender. Drain and cool slightly.

2 Remove the corn kernels from the cobs with a sharp knife or fork and grind coarsely. Add all the other ingredients to the ground sweet corn and mix well.

3 Rinse the reserved husk and dry on absorbent kitchen paper. Spread about 1 tablespoon of the mixture on one half of each husk and fold the other half over to enclose the filling.

4 Heat a heavy-based frying pan and grease lightly with ghee. Cook the stuffed corn husks on both sides until the filling has set.

7 Dot with butter and serve immediately with the chutney.

Moong Dal Handvo

Serves 4

350 g/12 oz moong dal
2 tablespoons oil
2 onions, chopped
2 carrots, chopped
225 g/8 oz cabbage, chopped
$\frac{1}{4}$ teaspoon monosodium glutamate
salt to taste

2 tablespoons natural yogurt
1 teaspoon bicarbonate of soda
2 tablespoons chopped fresh
coriander leaves
6–8 green chillies, chopped
juice of $\frac{1}{2}$ lemon
pinch of asafoetida

1 Soak the moong dal for at least 5 hours or overnight. Grind to make a coarse paste.

2 Heat the oil, add the onions, carrots, cabbage, monosodium glutamate and salt to taste. Cook for a few minutes.

3 Stir the yogurt, bicarbonate of soda, chopped coriander, chillies, lemon juice, asafoetida and salt to taste into the moong dal paste. Add half the cooked vegetables, mix well, then leave to stand for 10–15 minutes.

4 Spread most of the remaining vegetables in the base of a greased ovenproof dish. Spread the moong dal mixture on top. Finally cover with the last of the vegetables. Cover and bake in a hot oven (200 C, 400 F, gas 6) for 40–45 minutes.

5 Turn out on to a serving dish and serve hot with buttermilk (if liked).

Overleaf *From the left: Potato Roti (page 82), Cucumber Salad (page 74) and Masala Gobhi (page 39)*

Moong Dal Pudas

(Illustrated on page 61)

Makes 24

450 g/1 lb moong dal
200 ml/7 fl oz buttermilk
3 large tomatoes, finely chopped
1 small cucumber, finely chopped
5 green chillies, finely chopped
3 teaspoons chopped fresh coriander
leaves

$\frac{1}{4}$ teaspoon turmeric
pinch of asafoetida
salt to taste
butter or ghee for cooking

1 Soak the moong dal in cold water to cover for at least 5 hours. Grind coarsely and place in a bowl.

2 Add the buttermilk, tomatoes, cucumber, chillies, coriander, turmeric, asafoetida and salt. Mix well and set aside for 1 hour.

3 Grease a non-stick griddle or frying pan. Drop large spoonfuls of the mixture into the pan and cook until lightly set and browned on the underside. Turn over and cook until browned on the second side. Serve immediately.

Moong Dal Tikkas

Makes 10

225 g/8 oz moong dal
4 green chillies
100 g/4 oz white cabbage, chopped
1 onion, chopped
pinch of asafoetida
1 tablespoon gram flour
$\frac{1}{2}$ teaspoon bicarbonate of soda

$\frac{1}{2}$ teaspoon lemon juice
1 tablespoon chopped fresh
coriander leaves
salt to taste
butter or ghee for cooking
mango chutney to serve

1 Soak the moong dal overnight in cold water to cover.

2 Next day, grind the dal with the chillies. Add the cabbage, onion, asafoetida, gram flour, bicarbonate of soda, lemon juice, chopped coriander and salt to taste. Set aside in the refrigerator or a cool place for 1 hour.

3 Form small spoonfuls of the moong dal mixture into balls about the size of a large egg, then flatten them to form small patties.

3 Grease a non-stick frying pan with a little butter or ghee and cook the patties a few at a time, turning once, until browned on both sides. Serve hot with mango chutney.

Cabbage Wadas

(*Illustrated on pages 52/53*)

Makes 8–12

450 g/1 lb gram dal
7–8 green chillies
450 g/1 lb cabbage, shredded
1 carrot, finely chopped
1 onion, finely chopped

salt to taste
2 tablespoons chopped fresh
coriander leaves
oil for deep frying
Green Chutney (page 77) to serve

1 Soak the gram dal overnight in cold water to cover.

2 Set aside about a quarter of the soaked dal. Grind the remainder with the chillies. Add the cabbage, carrot, onion, salt to taste and chopped coriander to the ground dal along with the remaining gram dal.

3 Take spoonfuls of the mixture and knead into small thick cakes measuring 5 cm/2 in. in diameter.

4 Heat the oil for deep frying to 180 C/350 F, add the cakes, a few at a time, and cook until golden. Drain on absorbent kitchen paper and serve immediately with green chutney.

Overleaf *From the left: Paneer and Coconut Balls (page 114), Malai Pudas (page 117) and Bundi Laddoo (page 116)*

Rice and Cheese Balls

Makes about 20

75 g/3 oz long-grain rice	4 tablespoons grated Cheddar cheese
300 ml/$\frac{1}{2}$ pint water	$\frac{1}{2}$ teaspoon mustard powder
salt to taste	BATTER
3 tablespoons plain flour	200 ml/7 fl oz water
2 green chillies, chopped	50 g/2 oz plain flour
2 pinches bicarbonate of soda	ghee or oil for deep frying

1 Place the rice in a saucepan, pour in the water and add a little salt. Bring to the boil, then cover the pan, reduce the heat and cook for 25–30 minutes or until all the water is absorbed. The cooked rice should be sticky.

2 Mix the rice with the flour, chopped chillies, bicarbonate of soda and salt until the ingredients bind together.

3 Roll small spoonfuls of the mixture into balls about the size of a walnut, then flatten each to form a round shape.

4 Mix the grated cheese with the mustard and place a little in the middle of each rice cake. Carefully fold the edges over the cheese and roll into a neat ball, enclosing the cheese completely in the rice mixture.

5 Gradually beat the water into the flour to make a smooth thin batter. Meanwhile, heat the ghee or oil for deep frying to 180 C/350 F. Dip the rice balls in the batter, then fry in the hot ghee or oil until golden brown.

6 Drain on absorbent kitchen paper and serve hot.

Stuffed Potato and Paneer Pears

(Illustrated on pages 88/89)

Makes 10

25 g/1 oz butter
1 onion, chopped
1½ teaspoons ground cumin
50 g/2 oz peas, cooked
225 g/8 oz paneer (page 122), chopped
3–4 green chillies, chopped
1 tablespoon chopped fresh coriander leaves
½ teaspoon garam masala (page 124)

½ teaspoon chilli powder
salt to taste
1 tablespoon arrowroot
450 g/1 lb potatoes, boiled and mashed
75 g/3 oz plain flour
200 ml/7 fl oz water
oil for deep frying
about 50 g/2 oz dry breadcrumbs

1 Melt the butter in a frying pan, add the onion and cook for 1 minute. Add 1 teaspoon of the ground cumin, the peas, paneer, chillies, chopped coriander, garam masala, chilli powder and salt to taste. Remove from the heat and allow to cool.

2 Add the remaining ground cumin, arrowroot and salt to taste to the potatoes and mix thoroughly.

3 Take spoonfuls of the potato mixture (about the size of a small egg) and shape into small round cakes. Mound a little of the pea stuffing in the middle of each. Bring up the edges to enclose the stuffing completely and form a pear-like shape. Chill.

4 Mix the flour and water to make a batter, beating thoroughly until smooth.

5 Heat the oil for deep frying to 180 C/350 F. Dip the potato shapes in the batter, roll them in the breadcrumbs, then fry in the hot oil until golden brown. Drain on absorbent kitchen paper and serve immediately.

Overleaf *From the top: Malai Pedas (page 114) and Chocolate and Vanilla Barfi (page 115)*

Sweet Dishes

When sweet dishes are served as part of an Indian meal, they are presented along with the savoury food and not as a separate course. However, if you like you can serve any one of these dishes on its own to round off the meal.

Alternatively, why not try serving them as a snack with tea or coffee? The recipes are quite rich in the use of milk and paneer, so they should be served in moderately sized portions. Very fine and expensive edible silver or gold foil is sometimes used to decorate Indian sweetmeats or special dishes, but it is not an essential ingredient. More often, chopped pistachio nuts or almonds are sprinkled over the prepared sweet.

Although some of the recipes may need a little extra care in their preparation, particularly for those who are unfamiliar with Indian cooking, the results certainly warrant the effort involved and the dainty sweetmeats will delight your family and guests.

Paneer and Coconut Balls

(Illustrated on pages 108/109)

Makes 30

450 g/1 lb paneer (page 122)
75 g/3 oz icing sugar
2–3 teaspoons rose water
$\frac{1}{2}$ fresh coconut
75 g/3 oz sugar
$\frac{1}{4}$ teaspoon saffron strands

1 teaspoon milk
edible silver foil for decoration
(optional)
4–5 pistachio nuts, blanched and
chopped

1 Grate the paneer into a bowl, add the icing sugar and rose water. Mix very well to make a dough.

2 Shape spoonfuls of the mixture into small round balls about the size of walnuts.

3 Put the coconut and sugar in a saucepan and cook for 10 minutes over low heat, stirring frequently. Cool.

4 Warm the saffron and milk in a small basin over a saucepan of hot water. Rub in until the saffron dissolves. Add the saffron milk to the coconut and mix well.

5 Coat the paneer balls with the coconut mixture, rolling them carefully in the palms of your hands.

6 Arrange the paneer and coconut balls on a serving plate and cover with silver foil (if used). Chill thoroughly.

7 To serve, cut each ball into two and decorate with chopped pistachio nuts.

Malai Pedas

(Illustrated on page 112)

Makes 18

generous 1 litre/$1\frac{3}{4}$ pints milk
100 g/4 oz sugar
2 pinches citric acid
3 teaspoons water
$\frac{1}{4}$ teaspoon saffron strands
2 tablespoons cornflour

4–5 green cardamoms, ground
50 g/2 oz almonds, blanched and
chopped
10 pistachio nuts, blanched and
chopped

1 Reserve about 3–4 teaspoons of the milk. Boil the remaining milk in a large heavy-based saucepans until it is reduced to half its original volume. Add the sugar and continue to boil for 4–5 minutes.

2 Dissolve the citric acid in the water. Add this solution very gradually to the boiling milk until it curdles slightly. This may require anything from half to the entire quantity of acid.

3 Warm the saffron with 1 teaspoon of the reserved milk in a small basin over a saucepan of hot water. Rub the saffron occasionally until it dissolves, then add to the boiling milk.

4 Blend the cornflour with the remaining 3 teaspoons milk until smooth. Stir in a little of the boiling milk, then stir the mixture into the milk in the pan.

5 Go on cooking and stirring until the mixture thickens. Add the ground cardamoms and mix well, then allow to cool. Chill thoroughly for several hours.

6 Using wet hands, shape the cool mixture into balls and put in decorative paper cake cases. Decorate with the almonds and pistachio nuts before serving.

Chocolate and Vanilla Barfi

(Illustrated on page 112)

Makes 18 pieces

450 g/1 lb khoya (page 123)
150 g/5 oz sugar
$\frac{1}{4}$ teaspoon vanilla essence

2 teaspoons cocoa
cochineal or pink food colouring

1 Mix half the khoya with half the sugar in a saucepan and warm, stirring constantly, over a low heat.

2 After 4–5 minutes, remove a small spoonful of the mixture and test to see if it forms a soft ball when moulded between the fingers. When the mixture is ready, remove from the heat and add the vanilla essence. Stir for 1 minute. Spread the mixture into a small baking tin and allow to cool.

3 Cook the remaining khoya and sugar in the same way, but after switching off the heat add the cocoa and a few drops of cochineal instead of the vanilla essence. Stir for a little while, then spread evenly over the vanilla mixture. Allow to set for 4–5 hours.

4 Cut into pieces and serve.

Bundi Laddoo

(Illustrated on pages 108/109)

Serves 6–8

250 g/9 oz sugar
325 ml/11 fl oz water
1 tablespoon milk
a few saffron strands
125 g/4½ oz gram flour
pinch of salt
2 pinches bicarbonate of soda

ghee for deep frying
1 tablespoon melted ghee
4 almonds, blanched and sliced
4 pistachio nuts, blanched and sliced
4 green cardamoms, crushed
edible silver foil for decoration
(optional)

1 Mix the sugar with 200 ml/7 fl oz of the water in a saucepan and put to boil. Add the milk.

2 Boil the syrup steadily until it reaches the soft crack stage: 135–145 C/270–290 F on a sugar thermometer. At this stage, a few drops of syrup dropped into cold water should form threads which are hard but not brittle.

3 Place the saffron in a small basin with a little water. Stand the basin over a saucepan of hot water and rub the saffron occasionally until the strands dissolve.

4 Add the saffron liquid to the syrup, set aside and keep warm.

5 Mix the gram flour, salt and bicarbonate of soda. Add the remaining water to make a thick batter.

6 Heat the ghee for deep frying to 180 C/350 F.

7 Drop small, even portions of the batter off a spoon into the hot ghee and fry until golden brown. The cooked bundis should be about the size of large peas. Drain on absorbent kitchen paper.

8 Put the bundis into the syrup and leave to stand for 10 minutes. Add the melted ghee, almonds, pistachios and cardamoms to the bundis and mix well.

9 Using a wet metal spoon, form the bundis into small balls on a serving platter. Decorate with edible silver foil and serve.

Malai Pudas

(*Illustrated on pages 108/109*)

Makes about 20

100 g/4 oz sugar
200 ml/7 fl oz water
½ teaspoon saffron strands
a little milk
2 teaspoons rose water (optional)

6 tablespoons single cream
4 tablespoons plain flour
ghee for cooking
slivered blanched almonds and
pistachio nuts to decorate

1 Dissolve the sugar in the water in a saucepan and boil for 5 minutes.

2 Warm the saffron with a little milk in a small basin over a saucepan of hot water. Rub occasionally until the saffron dissolves, then add to the syrup. Stir in the rose water (if used) and keep the syrup warm.

3 Make a thick batter by gradually beating the cream into the plain flour.

4 Smear very little ghee on a hot griddle or heavy-based frying pan and drop small spoonfuls of batter on it to make small pancakes each measuring about 5 cm/2 in. in diameter. Fry on both sides until golden brown.

5 Dip the pudas in the hot sugar syrup and serve immediately, decorated with almonds and pistachio slivers.

Note: These little pancakes are very similar to drop scones. When they are cooked, place the pancakes on a piece of absorbent kitchen paper and keep them warm while you use up the remaining batter. The batter can be prepared in advance but make sure that the mixture is not too thick by the time you cook the pancakes. If the batter is too stiff, then add a little extra cream or milk.

Khurmani Ka Mitha

Serves 8

450 g/1 lb dried apricots
175 g/6 oz sugar
4 tablespoons dried milk powder
$\frac{1}{2}$ teaspoon ground cardamom
a few drops red food colouring
(optional)

TOPPING
300 ml/$\frac{1}{2}$ pint double cream
3 tablespoons icing sugar
2 bananas, sliced
2 blanched almonds, sliced
2 pistachio nuts, sliced

1 Soak the apricots in cold water to cover for several hours.

2 Halve and remove the stones if the apricots are whole, then place the drained fruit in a saucepan with the sugar and a little water. Stir over gentle heat until the sugar dissolves, then bring to the boil and simmer for about 15 minutes or until the apricots are cooked.

3 Blend the cooked fruit in a liquidiser or press it through a sieve, then return the mixture to the saucepan and bring to the boil. Boil, stirring occasionally, for 5 minutes.

4 Stir in the dried milk powder and continue to cook for a few minutes until the mixture thickens slightly. Stir in the ground cardamom and a few drops of food colouring, if liked. Spread this apricot mixture in a greased ovenproof dish or small individual dishes.

5 To make the topping, whip the cream with the icing sugar and spread about half over the apricot base. Arrange the banana slices on top, then spread the remaining cream over.

6 Top with the almonds and pistachio nuts and bake in a moderately hot oven (200 C, 400 F, gas 6) for 10–15 minutes. Serve immediately.

Orange Sandesh

Serves 6–8

1.15 litres/2 pints milk
juice of 1 lemon
2 oranges
4–5 tablespoons caster sugar

1 tablespoon orange juice
4 almonds, blanched and sliced
4 pistachio nuts, blanched and sliced

1 Bring the milk to the boil stirring frequently. Add the lemon juice and stir gently, then remove from the heat and stir until the milk curdles. Set aside to cool.

2 Strain the curdled mixture through a sieve lined with muslin cloth. Squeeze out all the liquid, then leave the paneer under a heavy flat weight for at least 1 hour. Meanwhile peel the oranges and remove all the pith. Cut between the membranes in the oranges and remove the segments.

3 Knead the paneer thoroughly with the sugar, add the orange juice and mix well. Spread half this mixture to form a 13-cm/5-in square on a plate or dish and arrange half the orange segments on top. Cover with the remaining paneer, spreading it evenly on top.

4 Chill before serving decorated with the remaining orange segments, almonds and pistachio nuts.

Note: The combination of paneer and orange makes this a particularly refreshing sweet – ideal for serving after a hot and spicy main dish. In India, sweets are usually eaten with the main course. If you are planning a traditional Indian meal, follow one of the menus on page 12 and arrange all the food together on the table, then eat small portions at a time from each of the dishes.

Narangi Ni Basundi

Serves 6

1.15 litres/2 pints milk
6–7 teaspoons sugar

1 orange
4 tablespoons orange juice

1 Boil the milk and sugar together until it is reduced to one-third of its original quantity. Stir occasionally during cooking to prevent the milk boiling over, then set aside to cool.

2 Peel the orange and remove all the pith. Cut between the membranes in the orange and remove the segments. Add these segments with the orange juice to the milk mixture. Mix well and chill for at least 1 hour before serving.

Baked Paneer

Serves 6–8

1.15 litres/2 pints milk
juice of 1 lemon
3–4 tablespoons caster sugar
$\frac{1}{4}$ teaspoon saffron strands

a little milk
$\frac{1}{2}$ teaspoon ground cardamom
$\frac{1}{2}$ teaspoon grated nutmeg
4 almonds, blanched and sliced

1 Bring the milk to the boil, stirring occasionally. Add the lemon juice, remove from the heat and stir gently until the milk curdles and a bluish water floats on top.

2 Strain through a muslin-lined sieve, then hang the paneer in the muslin for at least 2 hours. Knead the paneer thoroughly with the sugar. Soak the saffron in a little warm milk, then rub it in to dissolve the strands.

3 Add the saffron liquid and cardamom to the paneer and mix well. Spread the mixture on a baking tray to give a thickness of about 1 cm/$\frac{1}{2}$ in. Sprinkle the nutmeg over and top with the almond slices. Bake in a moderate oven (180 C, 350 F, gas 4) for 15–20 minutes, then cut into pieces and serve hot or cold.

Basic Recipes

Within this short chapter you will find the key to success for many of the other recipes in the book. Instructions are given for making a vegetable stock and for preparing ghee. Follow the methods for boiling rice and dal to ensure that these staple ingredients are perfectly cooked. And it is well worth roasting and grinding your own spices for freshly prepared garam masala which is far superior to any you can buy ready ground.

Recipes for paneer and khoya are also included. These are two milk-based mixtures which may seem complicated to prepare if you are unfamiliar with Indian cooking; however, the recipes are so clear and simple that when you have prepared them just once you will feel quite confident enough to make them regularly.

Vegetable Stock

3 carrots
225 g/8 oz French beans
2 large onions (unpeeled)
2 large potatoes

2 large tomatoes
small wedge of cabbage
1.4 litres/2½ pints water

1 Roughly chop all the vegetables and place them in a large saucepan with the water. Bring to the boil, cover the pan and simmer steadily for about 2 hours.

2 Cool slightly, then press through a sieve.

Ghee

1 Melt a quantity of butter (225 g–1 kg/8 oz–2 lb) in a saucepan, then allow it to simmer until a clear yellow liquid is formed and a sediment settles in the base of the pan. This should take about 25 minutes.

2 Carefully strain the clarified butter through muslin, making sure that all the sediment has been removed. Pour into a container with a close-fitting cover.

3 When set, this milky-white or slightly yellow solid can be stored in a covered container for long periods without spoiling.

Paneer

Makes about 175 g/6 oz
1 litre/1¾ pints milk   juice of 1 lemon

1 Bring the milk slowly to the boil. Gradually add the lemon juice while stirring continuously, then continue to stir gently until the milk curdles.

2 Set aside to cool, then strain the curdled milk through a muslin-lined sieve. Squeeze out the liquid (whey), then press the paneer (curds) under a heavy flat weight for at least an hour.

3 Cut into rectangular pieces or use as directed in the recipes.

Khoya

Makes about 225 g/8 oz
1.15 litres/2 pints milk

1 Bring the milk to the boil in a large heavy-based saucepan. Reduce the heat and simmer the milk, stirring frequently, for about 40–45 minutes.

2 The milk should be reduced to about a quarter of its original volume. When ready, the khoya should resemble a ball of sticky dough. It is used for making Indian sweets or as an ingredient in rich vegetable dishes.

Boiled Rice

Use long-grain rice for the recipes in this book. Basmati rice gives a better flavour in cooking and old Basmati rice is preferred for a good texture.

For pullaos

575 g/1¼ lb long-grain rice   1.5 litres/2¾ pints water

1 Wash the rice thoroughly under running water, then place it in a bowl, cover with water and allow to soak for 30 minutes. Drain.

2 Bring the measured water to the boil, add the rice and bring back to the boil. Reduce the heat and simmer the rice for 15–20 minutes. Take care that it is not overcooked and that the grains remain separate. They should not become mushy.

4 Drain the rice and allow to cool before use.

Note: For everyday use, use a generous 1.15 litres/2 pints water and cook the rice as above. Do not drain the rice but cover the pan and cook gently until the rice is cooked and the water has been absorbed.

Boiled Dal

to each 1 cup dal allow 2 cups water

1 Wash the dal under plenty of cold running water.

2 Place the dal in a saucepan with the measured water. Bring to the boil, reduce the heat and cover the pan. Simmer until the water is absorbed and the dal are tender – the cooking time varies depending on the type of dal.

Garam Masala

Makes about 1 tablespoon

3 cinnamon sticks   3 cloves   3 peppercorns

1 Grind the above ingredients together to form a powder. The quantities may be varied to suit individual tastes or for any particular recipe.

2 Generally, for home preparation, garam masala is ground in small quantities for immediate use. Freshly ground masala is usually stronger than the ready made varieties.

Punjabi Garam Masala

Makes about 2 tablespoons

2 cinnamon sticks	1 bay leaf
2 cloves	1 black cardamom
$\frac{1}{2}$ teaspoon cumin seeds	1 green cardamom
generous pinch each of ground	
coriander and ground cumin	

1 Roast all the spices together in a heavy-based frying pan over a gentle heat.

2 Stir the spices continuously until they are lightly coloured. They should give off a strong aroma when roasted.

3 Grind all the spices to a powder and store in an airtight container.

Glossary

Ajwain seeds Similar in appearance to celery seeds, with a strong, spicy flavour.

Aniseeds Small, brown and oval in shape, these seeds have a liquorice flavour.

Asafoetida A strong smelling powder with a distinct flavour, it is obtained from the gum of a plant and should be used only in small quantities.

Beans, black Small oval beans with shiny black skins.

Beans, dried broad Dried common broad beans, slightly brown in colour with wrinkled skins.

Beans, red kidney Fairly large oval beans with red skins. The beans should be boiled for 3 minutes to destroy natural toxins.

Cardamoms, black Large hairy pods which are black in colour. They are not as readily available as the green variety.

Cardamoms, green Pale green pods about the size of small peas, they are used either whole or the small seeds are extracted and ground.

Chick peas Small, creamy-coloured and similar in appearance to hazelnuts, these pulses have a nutty flavour. Also known as garbanzos and available canned.

Chillies Either green or red, chillies vary in strength but the seeds are always hot and should be removed if you prefer mild dishes. The following types are usually available:

    dried red Small wrinkled hot red chillies.

    green Fairly small chillies that vary in strength depending on the type. Generally, the long wrinkled chillies are very hot while the small plump ones may be either hot or mild.

    mild red Small plump Kashmiri chillies that are rounded in shape and not as pungent as the long wrinkled varieties.

    red Wrinkled, long red chillies or short and slightly plump with a fiery taste.

Cinnamon sticks Curled thin pieces of bark from the cinnamon tree. They are about 10 cm/4 in long with a strong smell and flavour.

Coriander leaves The fresh leaves look like feathery parsley and are sometimes sold as Chinese parsley. They have a pungent smell and strong flavour.

Coriander seeds These seeds are small, pale and round. They are used either whole or ground.

Cumin seeds White or black, these small long seeds are used either whole or ground.

Curry leaves Small, dark green and shiny, these leaves of neem trees are sold dried and are sometimes available fresh. Fresh curry leaves should be used if available and bay leaves may be substituted.

Dals These are skinned and split pulses.

Fenugreek leaves These are used as a vegetable in Indian cooking or they are sometimes added in small quantities to flavour dishes. They are sometimes available fresh from small Indian greengrocers.

Fenugreek seeds Small hard seeds, dull yellow in colour and almost rectangular in shape, they are used either whole or ground. They have a bitter taste.

Garam masala This is a mixture of spices ground together (page 124).

Ghee Clarified butter (page 122). Available in cans from small specialist shops.

Ginger, fresh root This is a tough, fibrous root with a fairly thick skin. It can be grated on a coarse grater.

Gram flour Either Bengal gram flour or chick pea flour, also known as besan.

Khoya Milk which has been boiled until thick and condensed (page 123).

Mango powder This is a sour powder which is made from dried raw green mangoes.

Masoor dal Skinned and split red lentils.

Moong dal Skinned and split mung beans.

Paneer Indian cream cheese (page 122).

Tamarind The dried pods of the tamarind tree, they are black and sticky with a sour taste. Tamarind paste is also available from specialist shops.

Toovar dal Skinned and split red beans.

Urad dal Skinned and split black beans.

Index